What Peo

"This poignant memoir of on(horses will inspire others to heed their heart's can to action. Nancy Lee Gerson is a gifted storyteller."

–Joe Camp, best-selling author of *The Soul of a Horse-Life Lessons from the Herd*, writer and director of five Benji films.

"At a Women's Quest™ horse retreat, the author fell in love with the horse she rode. Beyond this, she learned the exquisite lesson that when you open the heart, the heart opens you. *"The Horse Who Changed My Life"* is the story of a Heroine's Journey, one in which the author kindled the courage needed to heed the beckonings of horse and heart. Many people talk about making drastic changes in their lives, but Nancy Lee Gerson did it. Her recounting of her Aha, or Soul Spark, moments, during the retreat and in the years that followed, will inspire readers to hold fast to their dreams, visions and desires, and to the hope that each of us can take the first step in our own quests for inner freedom and happiness. This is a must-read book."

–Colleen Cannon, founder of Women's Quest

"'The Horse Who Changed My Life' is a lovely story that shows the transformative power of relationships with animals in our lives. The author's love of animals is always evident in this story of the magic that evolved from opening her heart to animals."

–Elizabeth Fulton, author of *Animal Reiki: Using Energy to Heal the Animals in Your Life*

"Nancy Lee Gerson is a passionate storyteller who draws the reader into her journey filled with fun and emotionally moving synchronistic tales. Her journey into full partnership with horses in her life, as an adult, speaks volumes illustrating her deep compassion for the spirits of both humans and horses. A delightful read."

–Melisa Pearce, founder of Touched by a Horse, Inc., author of *Equusology*

"'The Horse Who Changed My Life,' whisked me away into an amazing tale of love, following intuition, slow downing, and enjoying every step of the journey. This real-life adventure inspires one to believe that anything can happen when you have a dream and the courage to make it happen. The author's retelling of her saga took me from tears of sadness to tears of joy, and just about every emotion in between. This book will reignite one's love of nature and animals, including the horse, now more mystical to me than ever. Everyone in search of clarity on their own path should read this book."

–Mike Messeroff, Happiness & Personal Freedom coach, author of
"Dogs Get It, Advice I Learned from My Best Friend"

"An invitation to notice...In *'The Horse Who Changed My Life,'* Nancy Lee Gerson weaves together what seem to be wildly unrelated threads of the heart. Her choice to notice and then act upon a tiny thread from the heart of a horse, leads her on one heck of a cross country Spirit Ride. Readers on this journey will discover how threads from rock and roll lyrics, friends & family, and animal companions weave together to alter the course of her life. A true inspiration for all who share a heart connection with animals."

–Michelle Griffith, animal communicator,
founder of Mane Rise Pets

"A lovely, heart-filled story of a woman who leaves home and discovers the sacredness that comes from living in accordance with The Way of the Horse. I am humbled to have played a small part in the author's quest. "

–William L. Pelkey, Ph.D., founder of Equigetics™

"Nancy Lee Gerson is a gifted writer of story, poetry and song. Her words strongly resonated with me and created gorgeous scenery in my mind throughout the entirety of her journey. Vivid descriptions of her relationship with her four-legged companions clearly depicted the healing power of Equus and the magical connections made when our

The Horse Who Changed My Life

My Serendipitous Journey through Equus

The Horse
Who
Changed My
Life

My Serendipitous Journey through Equus

Nancy Lee Gerson

R

REDDER ROAD PRESS
Pine Bush, New York

The Horse Who Changed My Life: *My Serendipitous Journey through Equus*
Nancy Lee Gerson
Copyright ©2021 by Nancy Lee Gerson

Some names of persons have been changed in this book to respect the privacy of individuals.

The section titled, "Saint and Tamara" was previously published in Touched by a Horse Equine Coaching Stories, vol. 1

ISBN: 978-1-7371882-0-9 (paperback)
ISBN: 978-1-7371882-1-6 (ebook)
Library of Congress Control Number: 2021910348

Editing by Melanie Mulhall
www.DragonheartWritingandEditing.com

Cover art and design, Book design, Illustration by Hannah Chavez
www.hannahchavezart.com

Photographs by Elizabeth Chavez

First Edition
Printed in the United States of America

R
REDDER ROAD PRESS
Pine Bush, New York

www.nancyleegerson.com

Dedicated to my animal relatives, here and gone:
Lady, Roger, Jenna, Snuggle, Midnight, Duque, Ringo, Sammy,
Billy, Cherokee, Saint, Stitch, Dahli Lama, Leo, Mowgli, Choco,
and any animal relatives with whom I may yet join journeys
should my heart once again open wide and say, *Ahh*.

May all be happy.

May all be free from disease.

May all beings have well-being,

And none be in misery of any sort.

May peace and peace and peace be everywhere.

from the *Brihadaranyaka Upanishad*

Contents

Equestions

Will you be my easy keeper—
Filling up on the joy I'll feed you?
Be nourished by love, dive deep and deeper
Into the peace that this will lead to?
Will you graze upon my love by day, by night
And gorge upon my delight?
Feast upon my adoring sighs
Get drunk on the tears in my eyes?
Will you be my easy keeper,
Filling up on the joy I'll feed you?
Be nourished by love, dive deep and deeper
Into the peace that this will lead to?

Nancy Lee Gerson

1

Everything Will Feel Better
in the Morning

The farmhouse was completely empty—nothing but space and walls. I don't know what else I was expecting. Still, the moment I walked into the bare living room with Elizabeth close behind, I felt nothing. We dropped the bags and suitcases we were holding and stood there in silence. After a few moments, the chill in the room registered. It was late November, and there was no heat running through the baseboard radiator.

As we walked through the downstairs rooms, I knew I should be feeling some sort of excitement, or at least I *thought* I should be feeling that. After all the months of anticipation, where was the adrenaline rush, the heightened awareness?

This Colorado farmhouse property was a huge part of why I had given up a thriving law practice in Queens, New York, sacrificed proximity to family and friends, and effectively dissolved The PreCambrian Rabbits, a band I'd cofounded two years earlier. But most dramatically, I had walked away from a marriage that had lasted over two decades. Throughout that time, Luis had been a loving and devoted husband and an exceptional father.

1

We had known much happiness together as well as our share of challenges. One of the challenges was financial strain, though it was not for lack of strenuous effort on both of our parts to improve that aspect of our life together. I had gone to a retreat in Colorado, and two days after my return, Luis left for a nine-day meditation retreat. I hadn't told him about my decision to move to Colorado before he left, and even after he'd been back home a couple of days, I was still emotionally unready to tell him. Finally, though, I called him one afternoon after my court appearances were done and asked him to meet me for lunch at a local diner.

Once we were seated, he told me he had some ideas about how to alleviate at least some of our financial difficulties. I told him that I had something important to tell him too. He spoke first, and then it was my turn. I told him that I had decided to move to Colorado and that my plan was to be out West sometime within the next few months. Neither of us said very much after that. Instead, we left the diner together, walked out to our cars, and drove home.

For the next few months, we treated each other respectfully. There were no angry outbursts or accusations, but the mood was somber. At the same time, I was extremely busy with court appearances, client reports, and preparations for the move. It was a challenging time.

Still, I had made my decision, and Luis was generous in making things as easy for me as he could. When I left, I knew we would always be in each other's lives, not merely because we had children together, but because I hadn't stopped loving him. I just needed to heed the spiritual imperatives that had so clearly presented themselves.

And now this was it. The big moment had arrived, and I was sharing it with my beautiful twenty-two-year-old daughter who had volunteered to make the eighteen-hundred-mile trek to deliver me to my new home. Our other daughter, Hannah, was still in college, and there wouldn't have been room in the jam-packed car for three people anyway. It had been an extremely long trek. We left Queens early on November 27, 2010, and made it to Longmont, Colorado, about thirty hours later, at four in the morning. We made a stopover in Indiana, where we snuck Billy, our lab hound, and our two sister cats, Snuggle and Midnight, into a Motel 6 for a few hours of sleep. Apart from that, we drove straight through. The last few hours of driving in relentless high winds and darkness had been mentally, physically, and emotionally exhausting.

Was I flat-out depleted by some murky combination of driver's fatigue and numbness? Maybe that's what was going on with me. No. There was something else: deflation. Deflation without the slightest hint of excitement.

"The house is so cute, Mommy!"

I hope I smiled at that. I can't be certain. For a minute or so, all I could do was stand still and keep breathing. That was all the energy I could muster. I wanted to believe it was just the tiredness and the hour or even that painful sense of deflation, but my lack of energy and enthusiasm felt more profound than that.

"Before we go upstairs, maybe we should go back out to the car and get Billy and the cats," I said softly.

"Sure thing, Mommy."

Billy leaped out into the Colorado darkness and set about sniffing and zooming, zooming and sniffing. Midnight and

Snuggle meowed loudly as we carried them into the house and put them down in what I referred to from day one as "the cat room." We decided to bring in only a few blankets, towels, and pillows to use as makeshift bedding and leave the rest of the unpacking for the morning and went upstairs with Billy charging ahead of us. More sniffing, less zooming. When we reached the family room at the top of the stairs, we dropped our makeshift bedding down on the shaggy rug and looked around. Still wholly uninspired to say anything, I stood there mute while Elizabeth went down the hall to check out the three bedrooms and the bathroom. I was standing in the same place when she rejoined me.

"Maybe we can just sleep out here?" I said, more as a question than a suggestion.

"Um, sure," she replied.

We placed the oversized towels next to each other, arranged the blankets and pillows, and settled down to sleep. I started to weep. Elizabeth asked me what was wrong, and when all I could offer in response was my muffled crying and the soft heaving of my shoulders, she reached over and pulled me close to her. We lay there face-to-face, and for several horrible seconds, I was completely disoriented. *Why am I here in this room? What am I doing here?* My being there, in that room, in that house, didn't make any sense to me.

The word *panic* flitted into my head. That was it. I was in some sort of panic mode. Naming what I was feeling penetrated the numbness and snapped me out of the daze.

"Let's just go to sleep, Mommy. Everything will feel better in the morning," she said and planted a kiss on my forehead.

As I lay tucked inside the curve of her body, I felt comforted and protected. Hadn't I said those same words to her and her sister on many occasions over the years? Now that same time-tested counsel was flowing from daughter to mother. It was a poignant full circle experience—the first of many I would have on the serendipitous journey I'd begun. And though I'd never been able to fall asleep in an embrace, I did that night—or rather, that early morning.

Sure enough, everything *did* feel better in the morning. I woke up feeling refreshed, though still a bit achy, no doubt from the white-knuckled driving I'd done in those final hours. I rubbed my eyes, looked over at Elizabeth, and tried to recall any dreams I might have had. I didn't remember my dreams all that often, but I wondered if I had, perhaps, dreamt of Cherokee. Nothing registered, though, so I stood up and stretched. Soon I would be seeing my sweet fellow in the flesh, not in a dream.

2

Saddle Up Your Spirit

As I waited for Elizabeth to wake up, I thought back to that June evening, a few months earlier, when a horse had come to me—not in a dream but in a song. I couldn't recall ever having dreamt or written songs or stories about horses before that evening. But there it was, written down in my notebook, a fully composed song I'd just written about a rider flying through the night on a black stallion, gathering tales to be told.

Spirit Ride

A bridle of gold upon a black stallion,
A thing of beauty to behold;
But without a rider flying through the night,
There are no tales to be told.
Always longing to join in the race,
Hovering at the starting gate;
A moment of doubt can rob a soul
Of deep-down certainty, you . . . hesitate.

Saddle up your spirit, ride high and free and true,
Saddle up your spirit, that pulsing joy is you,
Saddle up your spirit, the winning's in the ride,
Saddle up your spirit, no need to stem the tide.
A bridle of gold upon a black stallion,
A thing of beauty to behold;
But without a rider flying through the night,
There are no tales to be told.

A week earlier, I drove to Fur Peace Ranch, Jorma Kau-konen's guitar camp in Pomeroy, Ohio, with my bandmate, Dave. Our guitar instructor for the next four days was Geoff Achison, an amazingly gifted Australian guitarist and sing-er. One of the tricks of the trade he taught us was the partial chord. Back in New York, I had sat in bed with my acoustic Taylor practicing some of those chords, and in half an hour, I had scribbled down the complete lyrics and score of what I immediately titled "Saddle Up Your Spirit." It was as if the song had written itself while I simply took dictation. I'd never written a song so quickly, and it was curious that I'd written it about a horse.

Two weeks later, I felt a strong desire to look into some sort of retreat. I scrolled online through three different cate-gories: nature retreats, silent retreats, and women's retreats. I was aiming for some time around the first week of August with Colorado in mind. I'd been there once before as a back-packing twenty-one-year-old. After a few minutes, Women's Quest®, an organization based in Boulder, Colorado, popped up on the screen. The founder, Colleen Cannon, led several types of women's retreats domestically and abroad. The one that called out to me was a five-day retreat in Colorado, taking place right within the time frame I had in mind for my getaway.

It was a horse retreat. Up to that point, my sole connection to the equine world consisted of a handful of nose-to-tail trail rides, plus several trips to and from Road's End Horse Camp in New Hampshire, attended by Hannah and Elizabeth for several summers. Growing up, I wasn't that little girl who dreamt of owning her own pony someday, and as an adult, I wasn't drawn to horses in an especially deep way. Admittedly, I enjoyed being introduced to the girls' favorite camp horses and watching their performances at the end of each camp session. And I had poignant memories of all those sad good-byes, telephone number exchanges, tender horse and human hugs, and the quiet melancholy that hung in the air for the first hour or so of the ride home.

I stared at the screen, contemplated briefly, and then dialed the number for Women's Quest. Colleen answered and told me there were still two spaces available. I immediately reserved one of them. Before hanging up, I mentioned that I was excited to pack up my guitar and get there. Colleen invited me to play for the group at the campfire gathering, which I said I would be thrilled to do.

The retreat was held at Peaceful Valley Ranch in the Indian Peaks section of Roosevelt National Forest, just outside Estes Park. Although I had never been to a dude ranch before, my first impression was that I had struck gold. There were gorgeous panoramic views, a main lodge that was large yet homey, and a group of very friendly-looking women. All told, there were sixteen of us, plus Colleen and her sister Kat.

I opted for a single room. An extrovert by nature and temperament, I was sure I'd enjoy everyone's company during the retreat. But I also knew that I would crave a quiet room to repair to, whenever I felt the need for solitude. We were given an attractive *WQ Journal* with poems, whimsical illustrations, coaching questions, and "stem sentences" sprinkled throughout its pages that were meant to stir our creative juices. I figured that some of the inspirational devices would work for me better than others. And being a longtime journaler, I also knew that I would probably cover page margins with aspirations, awarenesses, visions, and poems.

After everyone had checked in, we ate a hearty lunch and then gathered together in another room, seating ourselves around two long tables. As Colleen waxed exuberant about all the activities on the agenda for the coming days, I listened intently. I really did. But at the same time, I was thinking, *Yes, yes, that all sounds great. But when do we get to meet the horses?*

She picked up an oversized deck of cards and walked around the tables, inviting each of us to pick a card and read it aloud. They were beautifully designed with horse illustrations on one side and elegantly calligraphed words on the other. We would repeat this exercise of picking a card and reading it aloud every morning.

After the card ritual, Colleen asked us to share a bit about our previous exposure to and experience with horses. Some retreat participants were advanced riders, others were fairly amateur, and a couple had never even been near a horse. For

some reason, despite my being a very inexperienced equestrian, I told Colleen that I felt confident being put in the more
advanced of the two riding sections.

I was assigned a dark bay gelding named Cherokee with the
softest, hugest brown eyes I'd ever looked into. His mane and
tail were jet black with hints of rich coppery tones. He was very
handsome and not the least bit jittery when stroked. I loved
Cherokee on sight. In between our twice-daily riding sessions,
I hung out with him as much as I could, sneaking into the shed
for the garlic treats he loved whenever I thought I could get
away with it.

Thank goodness Colleen had taken me at my word about
my somewhat inflated equestrian experience. I suppose we both
took leaps of faith. Invisible threads were snaking up and down,
across and over, weaving the tapestry of my new life. Perhaps
the choices Colleen and I had made were spun from just such
threads. Whatever forces were at work and at play, I am forever
grateful that they brought Cherokee and me together.

3

Seminal Experiences with Cherokee

On the second or third day of the retreat, we rode up to a large open clearing, and Colleen directed us to bring our horses around to form a wide circle. As usual, she was beaming. With arms outstretched, she shouted, "Guess what's on the agenda, ladies? Yoga on Horseback! Awesome!"

When I guided Cherokee into position in between two other human-equine couples, it was such a smooth operation that it felt like I was parking a car. Sitting atop Cherokee in the early morning Colorado sunshine, it felt glorious to watch everyone move through yoga postures together. Cherokee was as calm as could be, the picture of equanimity throughout with no jigging or turning his head around to ask what the heck was going on up there. I felt thoroughly secure as I moved through the asanas. That experience of freedom, trust, and unity with Cherokee inspired a poem.

Equestrian Yoga (for Cherokee)

Bring your horse to a gentle stop,
Upon a Rocky Mountaintop;

Reach for the sun: Embrace, Release!
Rest together in universal peace.
Stretch to the left, to center, to right
Open your eyes, thankful for sight;
Your bodies united, grounded on earth:
A message arises: Each moment rebirth.
Thank your horse for holding you steady,
And sharing in Yoga Prayer Time;
No creature is more willing to stand at the ready:
No creature's company is more sublime.
Invite your horse to return to trail,
And take you back down and across the river;
He will do his best—In this he will not fail—
Acknowledge, with a smile, your awestruck shiver.
I thank you, Cherokee, for holding me steady
And sharing in Yoga Prayer Time
No creature is more willing to stand at the ready
No creature's company is more sublime.

That trust and unity I was developing with Cherokee kept deepening, and it led to a brief but seminal experience of tele-pathic interspecies communication one day during an outing to Beaver Dam. When we dismounted that day, the wrangler tied Cherokee and three other horses to a tree. Everyone else walked off in various directions, but I stayed behind and stood in front of the tree, admiring the horses. Cherokee was the furthest one to the left, with no horse on his right side.

I stooped to gather some nearby grass and offered it to all four horses. Then I moved over to stand next to Cherokee.

As I stroked both sides of his face and neck, over and over, I started to cry. After a while, Cherokee moved even closer to me, nudging right up against me. I murmured a thank you to him and allowed myself to continue weeping, not knowing if they were tears of joy or sorrow. But I knew enough to not risk limiting or changing what was happening by trying to analyze it. I just needed to honor whatever was taking place.

After I'd wept for several minutes, Cherokee moved away from me slightly. I stood there not understanding why he had moved away. *What is this about, and what is he trying to tell me?* I asked myself silently.

After several seconds, I heard the words *You're okay* in my mind.

At first I didn't get it. It was as though those two words had emanated from within me, and yet not. I continued to stand next to Cherokee with my hands at my side until, finally, I realized that it was a message from Cherokee. He was telling me that *I* was fine and that *everything* was fine. It was clear to me then that by moving himself slightly away from me, he hadn't dismissed me. He had simply brought our communion gently but firmly to a close.

I honored all of this knowledge, thanked Cherokee, and stepped back from him. As I looked around, the spell broke and I was brought back to the world at large. I saw the other ladies scattered about in little groups, eating their lunches. There was one lone lunch bag on the ground nearby, and I saw my name written on it. So I picked it up and went off to sit on a rock by myself to eat and let what had just happened sink in.

It wasn't until eighteen months later that I understood

more fully what had taken place between Cherokee and me, thanks to a webinar conducted by animal communicator and horse advocate, Anna Twinney. The theme was telepathic interspecies communication. In describing the many ways that humans can receive such transmissions, Anna mentioned that they often come through as words or phrases that arise in a person's mind. And she said that when messages come through in that particular way, the words most often sounded like that person's own voice.

It was so gratifying to hear that. I came away from the webinar with even greater certainty that what had passed between Cherokee and me was a telepathic experience. At the time, it had seemed odd to hear words in my mind in what sounded like my voice but which, I was certain, hadn't come from me. That experience with Cherokee was one of the highlights of the retreat: mysterious, mystical, and deeply rewarding.

But something else happened that day up at Beaver Dam Reservoir with Cherokee, something that filled the day with even more grace. While perched on that rock, eyes closed behind sunglasses and head tilted to the sun, I heard a voice ask, "Are you meditating or just resting?"

I opened my eyes to see a woman walking toward me. It was Jean. Right from the start of the retreat, there was an easy rapport among the women, and while I felt more simpatico with some women than others, I felt camaraderie with everyone in the group—except Jean. She was certainly pleasant enough, if a bit reserved, but I couldn't quite feel any connection with her.

I recognized that I'd just been gifted the perfect opportunity for precisely that. Patting the rock on my right side, I invited her to join me. We sat together in comfortable silence, bathing in the warmth of sunshine and kinship until the group was summoned by Colleen to mount up for the ride back to the ranch.

That sacred tree communion with Cherokee inspired a poem that not only expressed my certainty that he was my horse, but also pondered the question of how early on he knew that I was his person.

Cherokee (Cracked Wide Open)

Cracked wide open, under a Rocky Mountain tree,
Crying into the neck of Cherokee.
Tears flowing, all else disappeared,
Stroking and standing in oneness;
Love pervading, awash in unity:
Cherokee, how early did you know me?
Cracked wide open, under a Rocky Mountain tree,
Crying into the neck of Cherokee.
Swiftly now, swiftly we pair off,
Woman and Equus journeying forth
Swiftly now, not a moment will be lost:
All will align as a matter of course.
Cherokee, how early did you know me,
Know me to be the one?
Is it really all a timeless perfection:
Deeds to be done, in truth, already done?
I love you wholeheartedly, my equine mate.

Cherokee and I shared a wonderful riding experience from start to finish. Early on, he revealed his proclivity for speed and for moving up, unbidden, in his gaits. Given the choice, he liked to go fast. Still, I felt safe and secure with him. The trails in Roosevelt National Forest and Rocky Mountain National Park were often quite steep and craggy, and some of the trails had us riding very close to cliff edges. To my amazement, I stayed calm during those stretches. Was I attentive? Very. Scared? No.

Though my saddle was equipped with a horn, I knew it wasn't intended to be held onto as a security measure, nor as a mounting or dismounting aide. Historically, the saddle horn had been employed by riders working with their cutting horses to cut cattle. The saddle horn provided an anchor for the rider to tie or loop one end of the lasso rope onto; after successfully roping a cow or steer. I committed myself to staying off the horn, regardless of whether we were walking at an easygoing pace along level stretches, navigating cliffside slopes, or breaking into the occasional canter. Instead, I placed my trust in Cherokee's ability and intention to keep me in the saddle. It was exhilarating and profoundly satisfying to feel my body adjusting to move in sync with his assured rhythms. There was such intelligence flowing through our bodies!

On the morning of the last day of the retreat, I had another mystical experience, also under a tree. We had left the horses at the ranch and traveled, instead, by hayrack wagon up one of the mountain paths. We were invited to wander off into the nearby forest grounds and find places to commune in silence. After hiking for a short while and finding my spot, I lowered myself down to the base of a huge ponderosa pine, shimmied around until everything felt just so, and began sounding my mantra. At some point, the repeating beats fell away. I sat there with my eyes still closed, and after a while, I heard a sound that came from somewhere off to my left.

It was the distinctive sound of a horse blowing air through their closed lips. I heard it only once, but it was unmistakably equine. What was so striking about it was that none of our horses were nearby. They were tied up to trees on the other side of the expansive site we were on. I sat there a while longer and experienced a crystal clear knowing that I would move to Colorado and live with Cherokee.

Not long after that, while still leaning back against the ponderosa, I heard Colleen beckoning us in a sing-song voice. "Olly, Olly, oxen free! Olly, Olly, oxen free!"

We all came down from our respective spots and gathered together. She asked us each to share what our word or phrase of the day was, having spent some quiet time in the woods. As I listened to the other women, I practiced not searching for or rehearsing my own answer. When it was my turn to share, I spontaneously said, "Believe the vision," a phrase I'd never before uttered.

Then we formed a large circle and joined hands. Colleen stood in the center and began paying homage to the seven spiritual directions: East, West, North, South, Father Sky Above, Mother Earth Below, and the divine presence within. Next came the rope ceremony. We all took hold of a long strand of thin, gold-speckled blue rope and partnered up with the woman to our left. Walking around the inside of the circle, Colleen stopped before each couple and snipped off two small sections of the rope, one for each partner. Then we tied these cuttings, these "friendship bracelets," around each other's wrists.

Before bringing our ceremony to a close, Colleen gave everyone a silver "friendship token" about the size of a nickel and a tiny, odd-looking wooden gnome. We had each been given a small medicine bag, or amulet pouch, to wear around our necks when we first arrived, and we were encouraged to place in them things of value that we wrote, created, or found during the retreat. Coleen had started us off by giving each of us a tiny pewter angel. By this final day, my pouch was filled with meaningful objects and affirmations. I placed both the token and the gnome in my medicine bag, which had become very dear to me.

Then we were instructed to walk over to Angela. As I headed toward her, I felt gratitude for the sheer abundance of the day: the ride with Cherokee up to that lovely spot, the meditation and visioning under the ponderosa, the proclamation to believe the vision, the ceremonial circle, and now this next activity, whatever it was. Angela was holding out a huge ceramic bowl with tiny figurines of horses inside, of identical size and shape and in various colors. She referred to them as *fetishes* and invited each of us to take one. We gathered around the bowl and began choosing.

Naturally, I was hoping to select one that most closely resembled Cherokee. But by the time I had the opportunity to make my selection, none of the remaining fetishes were dark brown. Instead, I chose one—or rather, one chose me—with coloring that was a cross between light brown and orange. About an inch in length and half that in height, the marble horse was shiny, smooth, and soothing to the touch. It was precious. We stood around admiring our lovely gifts for a few minutes before putting them away in amulet pouches or pockets. Then we headed over to our horses to mount up and ride back to the ranch.

After we finished our final dinner together, we circled around a huge campfire for storytelling, wine, and music. When it was my turn to share, I recited a poem I'd written in my cabin the night before, titled "Questing."

Questing

The river is flowing: Are you going, are you going?

The ocean is wide: Are you open, are you open?

(Tell me,) are you open, are you open?

Life's dream is always waking: Are you quaking,

are you shaking?

The silent space within: Let's begin, let's begin (oh yeah),

Let's begin, let's begin (oh yeah).

Journey to the beloved, and find yourself, ah, hah,

Journey to the beloved, and find yourself, ah, hah.

Ride the river downstream: Swim the ocean's horizon;

Dream visions dance and flutter,

In a room glowing and humming. . .

In a room glowing and humming;

Realize that this is. . .the energy of your smile,

As you lie there in joyous. . .wonder, oh yeah. . .wonder, oh yeah.

Journey to the beloved, and find yourself, ah hah.

Journey to the beloved, and find yourself, ah hah.

After reciting the poem, I sang and played a few songs on my guitar, graciously accompanied by the crackling fire before me and the gushing creek behind me. I had to work pretty hard to make myself heard above the din of my "backing band," but it was a sweet dilemma.

Later that night, I laid my medicine pouch beside my pillow. The horse fetish tucked inside already felt special. In a series of events that unfolded over the next few years in Colorado, that horse fetish figured significantly in my life, and as it turned out, it was the perfect one for me to take home from the retreat. But the only perfection I was thinking about as I lay in bed after the campfire gathering was my new friendship with Cherokee.

Before falling asleep, I thought about how quickly and easily everything was falling into place since "Spirit Ride" had been written. It occurred to me that the genesis of that song, its inspiration, must have been rooted in something beyond the confines of my personal history. I knew a little about archetypes from fairy tales and other sources, and it seemed clear to me that those equine lyrics had come through so effortlessly because I had tapped into an archetypal energy field. There was a mystical connection between writing the song and meeting Cherokee. Intuition told me that the seeds of our joined journey had been planted with the channeling of that song, or perhaps even earlier.

4

Manifesting a Vision

I stayed in Colorado an extra day following the retreat as a gentle way to reimmerse myself into ordinary life. Besides, I hadn't seen Boulder since I was twenty-one. I decided to drive my rental car to the downtown area so I could have lunch somewhere on the Pearl Street Mall. I found a parking place and walked over to the meter, which I discovered only took debit and credit cards.

Up until then, I had never paid for parking with anything other than coins. I read the instructions for paying with plastic and was about to insert my card into the slot and became nervous about doing it. What if it got caught in the machine? I was in Colorado without much cash and no other credit or debit cards. Who would I call if my card got stuck? Quickly, though, I realized the irony and humor in my concern. *Oh my God. I just finished a five-day horse retreat during which I trotted, galloped, climbed up and down steep inclines, and rode near steep cliff edges. And I'm scared to put a piece of plastic into a little slot?*

I took the plunge and inserted my card. Then I walked a

short distance to a restaurant with outdoor seating and sat down at one of the outdoor tables. After ordering lunch, I took out my journal to jot down a few notes about the parking meter experience. I wrote about the fine line between fear and courage, hesitation and action. And I wrote about the connection I saw between the admittedly prosaic demonstration of courage back at the meter and all those horn-free, cliffside rides on Cherokee, up and down steep inclines and through tree-lined forest paths. Courage writ small and courage writ large, they all felt important sitting at the restaurant.

More than just acts of courage, those rides with Cherokee were magical and blessed, and it was bitterly hard to leave him behind when the retreat ended. Not only did I believe Cherokee and I belonged together, I *envisioned* us together.

Back in New York the first week of August, I was devoted to manifesting my vision. And Cherokee's. There was much to be done. By working feverishly, I took care of all the essential tasks in under four months. I set it in motion on three main tracks: reaching out to whoever Cherokee's owner was, figuring out how to support myself and various critters, and finding a place to live.

I learned the identity of Cherokee's owner within a day of my return to New York. Mark Bishop was one of the owners of Sombrero Ranches, one of the largest equine outfitters in Colorado. Several of his ranch horses had made up the group we rode at Peaceful Valley Ranch that summer. I called the ranch and was given Mark's cell phone number by one of the managers, but it took me three or four anxious days to reach him because he was in New Mexico with several Sombrero horses filming a movie on location.

Standing in my backyard in Queens, I called Mark, praying
that he would answer and that our telephone connection would
be good. He answered right away, and I explained why I was
calling. We exchanged a few niceties and then, to my enormous
relief, Mark expressed a willingness to sell Cherokee, but I still
didn't know how much he wanted for his horse. Emotionally, I
felt willing to pay *any* price for Cherokee, but financially, I knew
my limitations.

I braced myself for the next part of the conversation. As
I listened to Mark tell me what a great riding horse Cherokee
was and how he was still in his prime, I had to remind myself to
keep breathing. Fortunately, our amiable conversation came to
a swift and wonderful conclusion: He gave me his asking price
and I gave him my yes. I hung up and stood there in the yard,
tearing up with gratitude. The waiting and worrying of the last
few days were over. Now I could breathe easy in the certainty
that Cherokee and I would be together.

Next came the financial considerations. At the time, I had
a lively law practice. For the previous ten years, I had foregone
my own clientele and become a per diem attorney. My practice
consisted of handling court appearances and depositions for
other lawyers with scheduling conflicts. I was one of the per
diem "regulars," dashing up and down the steps of Queens
Supreme and Civil Courts every day, armed with paperwork
marked up with my scribbled notes. My days consisted largely
of conferencing several cases with judges and opposing coun-
sels and drafting stipulations and other types of agreements.
Most mornings found me sneaking in and out of courtrooms
trying to avoid being stopped in my tracks by the sound of the

judge's voice at my back saying, "Miss Gerson, don't leave my courtroom."

I made plans for another attorney to take over my per diem practice when the time came, including an arrangement whereby I would receive monthly funds from him. Then I researched how to waive into the jurisdiction of Colorado so I could practice law there without having to sit for that state's bar examination. I wasn't sure I wanted to practice law in Colorado, but I knew it was a good idea to secure the option to do so, just as a backup plan. That way, if the financial arrangements I was setting in motion didn't pan out, I would resign myself to living a double life, donning skirts and blazers in the halls of justice and Carhartts and mucking boots in the stalls of horses. Really, though, I envisioned myself cleaning up poop messes made by horses, not legal ones made by humans.

Lastly, there was the question of our home sweet home-to-be. I was guided by two key considerations: to board or not to board; Boulder or somewhere else. It took only seconds for me to realize how strongly I felt about having Cherokee at home with me. Just picturing him in a small off-site stall was an abdominal sucker punch. The second consideration didn't take long either. I had checked out Boulder after the retreat and loved the feel of the place, but I really wanted a rural property with barn, fenced acreage, privacy, and close proximity to Boulder. I pulled up a map of northern Colorado on my computer and soon set my sights on Longmont, a town a little more than fifteen miles northeast of Boulder.

My next stop was Craigslist. There it was, on the ninth page of ads, a posting for a hundred-year-old farmhouse with sixteen fenced acres divided up into several paddocks and pastures, a barn with four ten-by-thirty-foot outdoor runs, privacy, and rent I felt confident I could swing. Excited, I called the owner and arranged to see his property over the Labor Day weekend, since I was flying back then for Cherokee's prepurchase examination by a local veterinarian.

For the next month, as I awaited the Labor Day weekend, I carried my medicine pouch around everywhere. I even took it with me to court. Sometimes, while sitting in the pews waiting for my cases to be called, I would furtively take the horse fetish out and caress it while silently sending messages to Cherokee. *I'm coming back for you, Cherokee. I'll be there soon. Remember me. I'm coming back for you.*

When I arrived at Denver International Airport, I took possession of my rental car, drove to my hotel, and then immediately headed over to Sombrero Ranch. It was perfect timing because Mark Bishop was there all alone. I gave him an effusive hug, after which he walked over to a huge corral and started weaving his way through a throng of horses. There must have been at least two dozen of them in there, peacefully cohabiting. Finally, I spotted Mark walking back toward me with a lead in his hand. He had my boy!

He led Cherokee over to a vacant round pen and left me alone with him while he went over to chat with Mark Fitch, the veterinarian, and his assistant, Jenn. While brief, my reunion with Cherokee was soulful and sweet. Being able to see, smell, and embrace him again was delightful. I gave his nose a long stroke and quietly said, "I told you I would come back for you." And before leaving, I whispered to him that he would have to wait a little longer for me to come back again and take him to a place where we would be together every day.

Cherokee's prepurchase examination was a success, and I arranged for him stay put at Sombrero Ranch until my arrival in late November. I was extremely grateful and relieved that Mark Bishop agreed to let Cherokee sit out the upcoming September hunting expeditions.

Walking back to the parking area with Mark Fitch and Jenn, I gave them the abridged version of how Cherokee and I had come into each other's lives.

"So, you're moving out West for a horse," Jenn said when I'd finished. "Very cool!"

"Yeah, I guess I am," I replied after a moment's hesitation.

It was a little shocking, actually, to hear the obvious stated like that. I hadn't yet seen or acknowledged it to myself, let alone said it to anyone else. It was disconcerting how that simple, spontaneous exchange generated such a significant awareness.

After saying my good-byes to them, I called the owner of the farmhouse and got both the address and directions to the property. He told me to be on the lookout for a green street sign exactly one mile down the street that led to his property. At the sign, I was to turn left onto the dirt road, which was actually the long driveway leading to the farmhouse. Oddly, I didn't even know what name would be on that street sign. Either it was never mentioned or in all my excitement, I had failed to register it during the conversation.

It was a short ride to the farmhouse. I spotted the green sign from a distance and was impressed that it was precisely one mile down the street. As I slowed to make the left turn, I drew close enough to read the street sign. I was stunned. My soon to be new home was located on Journey Lane. *Journey Lane.*

I loved the house, the barn, and the whole expanse of property on sight. It was divided into several fields, all fenced and of varying shapes and sizes. There was an L-shaped corral around the barn, a yard surrounding the house on all sides, a sizeable rectangular field directly in front of the house, and two pastures of approximately six acres each (the "west pasture" and the "east pasture").

Everything more than lived up to the mental images I'd been conjuring from the posted photographs, and I could easily picture myself living there with my furry family. I sat down on the front porch steps and signed the lease on the spot. Later that night, I snuck into the hotel hot tub after hours and reflected on the day's events. Immersed in the swirling water, I felt a huge wave of satisfaction as I recalled showing Cherokee that I had kept my promise to him.

With the prepurchase examination and the leasing of the farmhouse squared away, I flew back to New York. Now I had to tough out another couple of months of being physically separated from Cherokee. I kept the amulet bag and horse fetish close at hand and continued to send loving messages to Cherokee. Fortunately, the days and weeks went by pretty quickly since I was well occupied, not only with my per diem law practice but also with the voracious reading I was doing about all things equine. I was educating myself about horse care, horse behavior, and generally what was involved in bringing a horse into one's life.

At the same time, I was also reading about subtler considerations, such as how horse and human interactions could bring about self-healing and mutual healing for both species. Before leaving Boulder, I'd stopped in at Lighthouse Bookstore on the Pearl Street Mall to see if I could find a book on bird "medicine" as follow-up to something that had come up during a private session at the retreat. Instead, I was drawn to *Horses and the Mystical Path*. After finishing that book, I delved into a book by Linda Kohanov, titled, *The Tao of Equus: A Woman's Journey of Healing and Transformation Through the Way of the Horse.*

I was spending as much time as possible immersing myself in the teachings, stories, and experiences of people who recognized horses as sentient, intelligent, peaceful beings who were highly articulate communicators, not only among themselves but also with humans. I was learning about two things that were especially enthralling to me. The first was that there were many people who believed that horses—The Horses in a collective consciousness sense—had been calling out to humans with cogent messages, expressing their willingness to teach humans how to live more peacefully and joyfully.

The other exciting thing I was reading about was the existence of specific methods and techniques for helping horses and humans heal one another and themselves through their interactions. The possibility of working with horses in a way that could facilitate that kind of synergistic exchange really lit me up. So, while poring over websites for guidance about horse care basics, I also made detours into articles and posts about various equine-related fields and professions.

One coaching program immediately grabbed my attention. It was the Touched by a Horse Equine Gestalt Certification Program® (TBAH). From the program's website: "The experiential nature of the method involves the horse as an active partner with the coach in the client's exploratory process. The integrative approach of the equine's interaction, combined with positive coaching, somatic awareness, guidance, and Gestalt methodology, assist the client in examining their life and choices made, with a focus on designing a positive future."

The website explained that the program required completion of a rigorous two-year course of study that included clinical hands-on experience. Upon graduating, students came away with knowledge and experience that not only enhanced their capacity to coexist harmoniously with horses on a personal level but also gave them the tools needed to start their own equine-related coaching businesses. And to top it all off, the program provided a built-in opportunity for students to do their own inner work and help their fellow students do theirs.

I wanted in! And as a further sign from Spirit that synchronicity and serendipity were supporting my vision, I saw that this particular program was not only located in Colorado, but it was right in Longmont! Boom. I sent my application in early November, enrolling for the semester that would begin in January, just weeks after my relocation to that very town.

Shortly before the move, I was driving down a road in Queens, New York, when a vow spontaneously arose in my mind as I envisioned Cherokee's arrival at the farmhouse: *I promise to honor you. I promise to respect you. I promise to give you the leadership you need and the companionship you crave as we journey forth together.*

I already had a strong intuition about why I had written "Questing." It was an ode to Cherokee: He was the beloved to whom I was going to journey to find myself. Our destinies were tethered together at the soul level. No wonder, then, that he was my muse right from the start, inspiring poems, odes, and vows—the tearful outpourings of my soul.

5

Saint and Serendipity

As the weeks went by, I continued speaking to Cherokee across time, space, and morphic fields, as much for my own sake as for his. Probably more. By silently reaching out in that way, I was ministering to a tender need to tug, gently but firmly, on the invisible cord that tethered me to my sweet fellow.

I knew that Cherokee had called me to him, and his beckoning had inspired me to write the song "Spirit Ride." He had summoned me to a new life, one that would align more authentically with the deepest needs of my soul. He was beckoning me to move on levels and in ways I could only partially see or understand, though my heart knew enough to make sure I heeded his call.

Around the same time, I came across a passage in a book about Rupert Sheldrake's work on morphic resonance. I knew he was a widely respected researcher and scientist who had studied dogs who knew when their humans were coming home. The passage I read elaborated on this theme, explaining not only that members of the same species could be affected by each other at a distance, but that *interspecies* emotional bonds could also be sustained over time and distance. This was made possible, he said, by a morphic field created when living creatures—of the same or different species—formed an emotional bond. The deeper the emotional connection, the stronger the morphic field. Those nonlocal fields could then act as a channel or means of communication.

Maybe I didn't need my brief telepathic communication with Cherokee validated or explained, but it was nice to have it anyway.

Elizabeth and I arrived in Colorado late that November and spent our first night in the farmhouse. And while I might have wondered what I was doing in Colorado in my exhausted state that night, I was very clear about it the next morning. I awoke, sat up, and had one immediate thought: *We have to go see Cherokee and pick out a companion horse for him!*

We fished out some fresh clothes from our suitcases, got dressed, and headed to Sombrero Ranch's farm operation over on Niwot Road, where the southwestern tip of Longmont met the small town of Niwot.

A few weeks earlier, I had made the decision to adopt a companion horse for Cherokee and had discussed it with Christy Cramer, who worked with the Sombrero outfit. During our telephone conversation, she suggested that I check out some of the horses the ranch planned to sell when I came back for Cherokee. She referred to them as "sell off horses" and explained that every November, Sombrero's owners and staff determined which of the horses were still sound but deserving of retirement from the rigors of the for-hire life. It also made good business sense for the ranch to sell those horses for a nominal fee, thereby avoiding the expense of wintering horses who weren't going to resume their work lives come spring. We agreed to meet at Sombrero Ranch and have a look at that year's available horses once I had moved into the farmhouse in late November. So *that* element of adrenaline was also coursing through me as we drove over to the ranch.

I was buzzing with anticipation and close to tears as we pulled into the parking lot. It was happening. I was going to see my Cherokee again, and he would see that, once again, I had kept my promise to come back to him. When we arrived, I introduced Elizabeth to Cherokee, and then we were led over to another huge corral. Christy told us that there were nine horses in the group of retirees that year, and they were presented to us one at a time.

After looking at the first eight horses presented, I fell in love with the ninth one and asked Elizabeth to ride him around the corral for two or three rotations. His gait was unhurried and steady. He was a handsome strawberry roan with a large head, round feet the size of saucers, and an incredible medley of hues in his blonde mane. He had highlights! He also had a large white blaze running down nearly the entire length of his face and white socks on all four legs. Shortly after adopting him, I learned that a horse who has four white socks and a blaze is sometimes referred to as a horse "with a lot of chrome," much in the same way as a car's silver trim might be described.

As Elizabeth rode him bareback around the corral for a few minutes, I took note of his quiet manner. He was the one. I wasn't told his name, nor did I ask for it. I kissed his neck and we left. Christy hauled Cherokee and The Nameless One over to the farmhouse by the next day. Within my first thirty-six hours as a Coloradan, I had rejoiced in two happy events: a housewarming and a horse-warming.

Christie and I both saw how calmly The Nameless One allowed himself to be touched, bridled, and saddled in unknown territory, then mounted and ridden by me—a rank amateur. She held the reins as I dismounted after my first ride on him. "Well, that was great. Our first ride together!" I said. "He's such an easygoing fellow, isn't he?"

"Yeah," she agreed. "He's a real saint. He really is."

In that moment, I knew Christy had just given me the perfect name for this gentle gelding. For the next few days, though, my bruised ego grumbled about the fact that I hadn't been the one to name him. But once I got over myself, The Unnamed One officially became Saint.

Released together into one of the paddocks, Cherokee and Saint began to graze the meager late fall pickings. Elizabeth and I were enjoying that peaceful sight, when the scene changed and we were treated to a captivating display as the herd's hierarchy was swiftly established. After the grazing had gone on for a while, Saint turned and began calmly walking toward the back of the barn. He came around the other side of it and just as he was about to walk into one of the runs, Cherokee charged over and blocked his access. With a snort as he left, Saint went back out to the paddock and resumed his grazing, as did Cherokee.

A few minutes later, Saint tried again to gain access to that same run, and once again, Cherokee overtook him before he could take more than a few steps inside it. There was another snort from Saint as he took his leave. Cherokee left the barn as well, and both horses went back to grazing.

As soon as Saint began his third attempt, I asked Elizabeth to hurry over to Cherokee and head him off at the pass. She distracted him with handfuls of hay long enough for Saint to make his way over to the four runs. But this time he chose the one to the right of the run he'd tried to enter on his first two attempts. Cherokee quickly left Elizabeth, came around the side of the barn, and walked briskly into the run that he had already declared as his own.

That was the first time I witnessed herd dynamics at work.

From my human perspective, the horses seemed to have made a seamless transition into their joined journey. They both knew where they stood in relation to one another, and their easygoing relations made my entry into human-equine cohabitation that much easier. I never asked Mark Bishop or any of his ranch hands whether Cherokee and Saint had spent any time together. All I knew was that for the past several years, they both had been dude ranch horses.

What made me pass on the first eight sell-off horses presented to Elizabeth and me? What triggered my yes to that red roan fellow with such certainty? No doubt, some of those invisible threads were warping and weaving away to join together Saint's journey with Cherokee's and mine.

After our first few hours of observing how peacefully Saint and Cherokee were getting along that first day, Elizabeth and I felt comfortable leaving them alone for a short spell. We drove out to stock up on some basic horse supplies. By a stroke of good fortune, Murdoch's Ranch and Home Supply was located right down the road. It was a mecca for all things equine. The shelves were chock full of bug repellents, fly masks, wound care products, and countless other items that had never before been on my radar. It was exciting and overwhelming at the same time. I had to focus on the few items I knew we were there to buy.

Horse treats were at the top on our list. We were amazed at the variety of choices available to us. As I was reading the label on a large jar of oat and carrot cookies, I heard a cheerful voice exclaim, "Oh, those treats are the best! My guys go absolutely crazy for them."

We looked up to see a vibrant redhead who introduced herself as Tamara. A native Coloradan, Tamara had rescued three horses from less than ideal living situations. She renamed them Star, Symphony, and Spirit. Despite financial stress, single motherhood, and a demanding work schedule, Tamara was devoted to her own equine trio. We chatted briefly in the store and then exchanged telephone numbers.

A week later, she came by my place to meet my menagerie, and then I followed her in my car to meet hers. She lived in the quiet town of Berthoud, about a half hour north of Longmont. After introducing me to her beautiful herd, she took me to a quaint store in the town's bite-sized shopping district. The place was filled with all manner of western paraphernalia and tchotchkes. The first object my eyes landed on was a sky-blue painted wooden plaque, a foot in length and a half-foot high, with the calligraphed words, "Celebrate the Journey." After seeing it, I had no desire to browse any further. I was already envisioning how the plaque would look hanging on my front door.

That was yet another message about taking journeys. Within the brief expanse of a year and a half, I'd been inundated with messages about going places. First, there was my song, "Spirit Ride," with its lyrics, "Saddle up your spirit, ride high and free and true." Then I went on the horse retreat and wrote "Questing," a poem with the refrain, "Journey to the beloved and find yourself." Next, I discovered the perfect rural property to rent, located on Journey Lane. And now this plaque. In a novel I'd read some time ago, one of the characters commented that she was living in "the oxygenated heart" of the word "almost." My word was "journey." I was living in the oxygenated heart of the word "journey."

Tamara quickly became my close friend. She also became my hair stylist. Each month, we got together at her place or mine to have pizza or pasta for dinner, after which she would cut and color my hair while we chatted or watched a movie. During one of those monthly pizza and hair coloring evenings, Tamara and I were looking at some photos taken by Dave, my bandmate from the PreCambrian Rabbits, during his recent visit. While looking at a shot of me standing in the field directly across from the farmhouse with my arms outstretched to Cherokee on my left and Saint on my right, Tamara exclaimed, "Oh, my God, Nan, this is what you drew! You drew Cherokee and Saint together! You see? Even then you knew. Wow!"

A few days earlier, I'd shown Tamara my Women's Quest journal. In it, she'd seen the primitive sketch I'd made of me standing between two horses with my arms outstretched to each one. I agreed with Tamara that the two horses were Cherokee and Saint, and then I flashed back to the retreat day when I'd meditated under that huge ponderosa tree. At the time, I'd experienced a clear knowing that I would move to Colorado and live with Cherokee. But now, staring at the photo with Tamara, more dots connected. My stick figure retreat sketch represented yet another vision I'd had while on retreat: I had foreseen the arrival in my life, and Cherokee's, of a second horse: Saint.

Saint quickly began living the life of a cherished and pampered retiree at my place. Only occasionally did I ask him to take me for short rides around or slightly off the property—barefoot, bareback, and bit-less. And even then, all but a scant few yards of those outings were done at more than a walk. Saint's best offering to me wasn't the solid expanse of his back, but the tender expansion of his heart. The most rewarding aspect of our joined journey was the way he softened to me and gained a capacity both to give and receive affection.

A few months after moving to Colorado, a horse trainer I had briefly engaged trailered Saint and me to an indoor arena in Longmont, to participate in his group riding lesson. At one point, while I was dismounted and standing with Saint, cleaning his tail, a woman rode over to me and struck up a conversation. I told her I had two horses, Saint, who was with me, and Cherokee. And I said they'd both been Sombrero Ranch horses. When I mentioned Mark Bishop's name, she smiled and said she knew him. We agreed that Mark was a straight shooter to deal with and extremely likeable to boot.

We chatted a bit longer, and when I got to the part about how I met Cherokee, she stopped me before I could finish.

"Oh, wow!" she exclaimed. "You're that woman from New York. Yeah, Mark didn't even want to sell that horse. But he said that a woman who rode Cherokee at some kind of retreat was so crazy about him that Mark agreed to sell him. You're her, aren't you?"

"Yup," I said. "That's me. Guilty as charged!"

It was true. During our brief telephone conversation, Mark told me that he wasn't even thinking of selling Cherokee, that he was a good horse who was still young and in his prime at twelve years old. I believed him. Even across distance and through fiber optic wires, I could hear that this was not just pre-sale posturing. Mark exuded honesty and decency.

In the end, I didn't continue working with the trainer who had trailered us to the arena that day. We weren't a good fit. Also, my horses and I never stepped hoof or foot into that arena again. Still, it was special that Saint and I were there that particular day to meet that particular woman. Sharing that bit of "right place at the right time" serendipity with Saint was certainly a memorable experience.

But I discovered another serendipitous connection Saint and I shared that went way beyond merely being memorable. It made me consider my horse fetish in a radical new light, and it also gave me a glimpse into how magical and mysterious the whole equine journey was.

Those insights came about when I was down on the Pearl Street Mall in Boulder one evening, listening to some music at The Laughing Goat. The musical fare at that cozy venue was mostly in the roots, bluegrass, folk, and Americana vein. I sat down at a table a good distance from the stage and opened up Linda Kohanov's *Riding Between the Worlds*. Having previously read her earlier work, *The Tao of Equus*, I was captivated by her insights into equine mind and spirit, as well as her navigation in deep archetypal waters.

While reading the book that evening, I had a jolting awareness. I looked up from the book and stared off into space, awash in the imploding aha. Then I packed up my things, hurried out to the car, scribbled a few notes, and drove home, spurred on by the need to look inside my amulet bag. But as soon as I walked into the house, I realized that I had no idea where it was. Several boxes still needed unpacking, and I was certain that I hadn't seen the medicine pouch since moving in.

I needed to take a good look at my horse fetish because down at the music venue, it had dawned on me that my choosing that particular one from the retreat bowl had been both serendipitous and synchronistic. I had wanted a fetish that matched Cherokee's markings, but since none were available when it came my turn to pick, I selected one with differently colored marble. Sitting there at the café, I realized that the fetish I selected had markings that, magically enough, matched those of the next horse who was destined to capture my heart four months later: Saint!

It was beautifully fitting that things had worked in that way. Back in New York, during the months leading up to the move, I had been in the habit of taking the medicine pouch with me wherever I went so I could take the horse fetish out to hold and caress. I did that even while sitting in courtrooms awaiting my turn to approach the bench. Running my fingers over it had offered both comfort and a sense of connection to Cherokee—or so I thought. At the time, I had no inkling of the larger significance that this particular fetish's presence in my life portended.

Standing in the farmhouse living room, I wondered where

to begin my search. Several boxes still needed unpacking, and I was certain that I hadn't seen the medicine pouch since moving in. Where could it be? I went upstairs and quieted myself to see if I could receive an image or other kind of message about the whereabouts of my treasured talisman. Very soon, I saw in mind a black bag lying in the closet of "the cat room." I hurried downstairs, spotted a black bag in the closet, and looked inside. No medicine pouch. Disappointed, I looked around at the other items in the closet and found the amulet pouch in a duffel bag nearby.

When I took the fetish out and held it next to a photo of Saint, I saw right before my eyes what had dawned on me down at the Laughing Goat: I had chosen a fetish that matched *Saint's* coloring. I had summoned him, or he had summoned me. Perhaps we had summoned one another. Now I understood, intuitively, that Saint had been making his way to me during all those weeks of taking that fetish out to hold and caress back in New York. It hadn't borne a resemblance to Cherokee because it hadn't represented him. It had represented Saint, though I didn't know it at the time. Even when I made the decision, a few weeks prior to moving out West to adopt a companion horse for Cherokee, I had no idea that out of all the horses presented to me at Sombrero Ranch, the one I would gravitate to would look almost identical to that fetish.

Despite the limits of my grasp of quantum principles, multiverses, and whirling whorls, it seemed clear to me that Saint and I had met in the serendipitous choosing of that retreat fetish, and that he had been pulling me to him in the months before we met in the physical realm.

6.

Magical Connections Added to the Mix

Serendipities, synchronicities, and magical connections were the through lines of my westward journey, beginning with the writing of "Spirit Ride," or possibly even earlier. There were so many moments when I had to grin and wonder about the divine timing of the events that were unfolding. I was definitely getting the message from Spirit: This journey was going to be chock full of lessons about much more than how to live with and care for horses. It was going to be a journey of believing the visions, as I had proclaimed at Peaceful Valley Ranch.

Scarcely a week after my move to Colorado, I was sitting at one of the high-top tables at Crane Hollow Café. I'd discovered the rustic eatery when I returned to Colorado for Cherokee's prepurchase examination and the farmhouse viewing, and I knew at once it would become my favorite breakfast spot / reading room / journaling nook.

I ordered my usual dish, the veggie scramble, and took out the questionnaire I needed to complete for my appointment later that morning with the head of the Touched by a Horse certification program. After answering the final question, I put the sheet back in my Women's Quest folder, which I was bringing to the meeting. I was all set to head over there when my inner voice told me to open the folder again and take out one of the cards I'd pulled from the deck while on retreat. They all had the illustration side faceup, and I couldn't recall what message was on the flip side on any of them. I chose one and admired the beautiful artistry before turning it over.

The card I picked was the one titled "Becoming A Student." The message was about how adopting a student mindset allowed you to become teachable so knowledge could flow in a receiving direction, rather than an offering one. Seeing that particular card on that particular morning was, in and of itself, wonderfully serendipitous. But that wasn't all.

Before putting the card back in the folder, I glanced down at the signature below the message. Had I not taken note of that during the retreat? Maybe yes and maybe no. It didn't look the least bit familiar to me. Either way, one thing was certain: Whether or not I'd previously been aware of the author's name at that time, I hadn't given any further thought to those cards or their creator once I was back in New York.

But that morning, I'd been drawn to open the folder and select one of the cards. What I saw blew my mind. The author of those exquisite cards was none other than Melisa Pearce, the head of the equine coaching program—the very person I was heading out to meet! I thought I'd be meeting her for the first time, but it seemed I'd already met her a few months earlier through the cards.

I sat there for a minute, taking in not only these remarkable connections but the serendipitous timing of it all. Then I paid my bill and drove to the appointment. When I got there, I sat down across from Melisa and, without saying a word, placed the student card on the table. Melisa looked down at the card, then back up at me, and let out a gleeful shriek. This was followed by our laughter and handclapping—and that was *before* I'd even shared with her the above-described magical sequence of events. I was accepted into the program for the next semester.

Divine forces had not only brought me together with Cherokee and Saint but had also led me to Melisa Pearce during my retreat, and soon after, to her training program. It promised to be an equally magical journey toward certification as an Equine Gestalt Coach. And even though the semester I was enrolled for was going to begin a mere five weeks after my arrival in Longmont, I trusted that this timing, too, was serendipitous and divine.

All of these events and encounters were huge clues for me that my life was being guided by spiritual and mystical forces that I didn't fully understand but knew I needed to keep honoring as my western adventure journeyed forth.

7

Dahli Lama

The serendipitous and mystical ways that horses were coming into my life wasn't over. And this time, Melisa Pearce had something to do with it. Some months after I joined the program, I read a post by Melisa on our closed-community Touched by a Horse Facebook page. She mentioned that there was a fourteen-month-old filly who was about to be culled from the herd up at a breeding ranch about an hour northeast of Longmont. Due to being pigeon-toed, or "toed-in" on her left front leg, she wasn't considered conformationally sound. The defect was either congenital or had occurred in utero. If the former, she was "unusable" as a broodmare. Therefore, the ranch owners were going to put her down if she wasn't adopted very soon.

At the request of a friend and with the aid of a photograph, Melisa engaged in telepathic communication with the yearling. She wrote that the young horse was highly intuitive and would make an ideal partner for someone's equine coaching business. Having experienced Melisa's animal communication skills firsthand, I trusted what she posted.

I knew I had to meet the young horse, despite the likelihood that a mixed bag of considerations was going to rise up.
There was what I called my Florence Nightingale complex,
which made me wish I could cuddle all injured creatures and
love them back to health again. And there was my entrepre-
neurial curiosity, which made me wonder if the filly *could* pave
the path to my successful equine coaching business.

But what about my knee-jerk, gut-punched emotional reaction to animal disability in virtually any form? No badge
of honor there. If anything, I considered it a weakness. Hannah and Elizabeth were always considerate about alerting me
whenever they posted on social media any content that exposed
animal cruelty or injustice. And their movie recommendations
often came with warnings that I would need to shield my eyes
during a scene or two. Did I really want to adopt a creature with
a physical appearance that might saddle me with sadness and
her with pity?

Ultimately, I made my decision the way I was making so
many others on my western adventure: by listening to the quiet
yet compelling need to heed my heart's imperative. And its bell-
clear voice said, *Go see that horse. Just go.* The next day, I drove
up to the ranch with Maarten, a friend from the equine coaching
program, who had also read Melisa's post about the horse.

The yearling was enchanting: diminutive in stature and
gorgeous in coloring with her blue roan coat and black mane
and tail. Her demeanor was calm yet curious. I knew I wanted
to adopt her.

"She has a huge heart," Maarten remarked as we walked
back to the car after our visit. We drove in silence for several

miles before Maarten admitted that he'd been quietly contemplating how *he* could adopt the filly. I was shocked and stung. I hadn't even considered that possibility. I thought he had come with me solely to offer another set of eyes.

His voice sounded near yet distant. Something was closing in on me, a vague sense of doom. I heard him say something about boarding the filly at my place and coming back from time to time to do equine coaching sessions, jointly with me, because he was living a rather nomadic life. And he said something about co-owning her with me. What the hell did that mean? I hated the term at once and would never have agreed to such an arrangement.

By then, it had grown dark. With a too-firm grip on the steering wheel, I let my eyes adjust to the headlights from the oncoming traffic, hoping that Maarten would attribute my silence to my need to focus on the road. In reality, I was a toxic blend of confusion, anger, and distress. I wanted to scream, beg, or drop him off at the nearest airport. Mostly, I wanted to cry.

We arrived back at my place and ate together in front of the television without discussing the filly. I offered him the spare bedroom if he wanted to sleep over, given how late it was and how long a drive he would've had. After he went off to sleep, I stayed up and vegetated on more TV, trying not to think about the uncertainty of our conjoined fates, the filly's and mine.

Maarten headed out the next morning. Happily, by that evening, he had changed his mind about adoption or co-ownership. He called to say as much and to offer me his blessing.

"I know you'd take really good care of her, whether she was yours, mine, or both of ours. But I think it's important for both of you to know that you belong to each other. So she's your horse, Nancy, if you want her. I think you should go for it. You're gonna do some great coaching work together."

I thanked the universe for keeping intact my freedom to share a joined journey with the lovely young horse. Two days later, I drove back up to the ranch to spend time alone with her. When I arrived at the ranch, there was nobody in sight. I called out a greeting at the entrance to the huge barn and peered down the long center aisle. No one answered or showed themselves. When I walked over to the office and tried the doorknob, it was locked, and there was no note on the door. It was unusual and even a little unsettling to come onto the property of a large ranching operation like that in the middle of the day and see no signs of human activity. I felt a bit like a trespasser.

At the same time, I was determined to stick around to see that yearling again. I went back to the barn and walked down the aisle to her stall. She greeted me with the same calmness and innocent curiosity she'd exhibited two days earlier. After stroking her nose and neck over the top of the door for several minutes, I lifted the latch and, somewhat furtively, went inside. Standing beside her, I noted that I was taller than her by at least a foot. Her head came up to my chest.

From what I could see, she moved about easily with no discernable limp. I moved slowly past her, giving her a wide berth to avoid spooking her, and walked out into the long outdoor run attached to her stall. She turned herself around and came with me, stopping when I did. What transpired over the next ninety minutes was a series of equine movements that I wouldn't have recognized, let alone understood, a few months earlier. But thanks to what I was learning in the equine coaching program just then, I knew what was taking place between us.

This lovely creature was an energy worker, and she was focusing her attention on chakras, hers and mine. We were being taught all about chakras: where in and around the physical body they were located; what each one represented; what colors and qualities were attributed to each of them; what it meant to say that a particular chakra was out of balance; and the methods for realigning them. Being taught that those vortices of energy pertained to equines and humans alike really blew the top off for me. And while it wasn't universally understood that horses knew how to recognize and realign chakras, Melisa Pearce was clear that all horses had that ability and taught about it in her program. She told us that horses who chose to align chakras in people usually worked both sides of a person's body. By that point in my training, I had already witnessed one of her horses, Fancy, do just that while working on my fellow students in the round pen in Melisa's indoor arena.

Like the proverbial bell that can't be unrung, equine energy work, once witnessed or experienced, cannot easily be denied or dismissed. And standing outside in Dahli Lama's run, I knew without a doubt that she was balancing my root and heart chakras. Her actions were intentional and precise. What this looked like was a series of slow and deliberate movements on her part as she offered me the areas of *her* body that corresponded to *her* root chakra and *her* heart chakra. To send healing energy from her heart chakra to mine, she positioned herself so the side of her body—specifically, the area associated with her heart chakra—was directly in front of me, aligning that part of her body with my chest. She did this with her left side.

After staying like that for a while, she then rotated her body so her rump—the area where her root chakra was located—was directly facing my chest. In that way, she was sending healing energy from her root chakra to my heart. After that, she repositioned herself so our respective heart chakras were once again aligned with each other.

And so it proceeded, with her moving back and forth between those two healing positions. While she barely touched my body with most of her movements and positionings, a couple of them were a bit more energized as she ground her rump into my chest for what seemed like several minutes. I remained silent and completely still, but for the flowing of my tears.

Finally, much like Cherokee had done under the Beaver Dam Reservoir tree, Dahli Lama moved slightly away, letting me know that she was done working on me. I thanked her and gave her a kiss before leaving, then hurried back to my car, anxious to record the experience while it was freshly imprinted in mind and heart. Sitting in the car, still teary, I journaled about the experience. I knew that our soul-seeds had just been sprinkled together into the same patch of sacred ground.

Dahli Lama: The newest member of my horse/dog/ cat/rabbit/human herd. I've just spent hours alone with her. She did alternating root and heart chakra work on me throughout our time together. Her root chakra movements were forceful in their intentionality a couple of times. Once, she moved her body around and backed up right into my front torso, causing me to take a step back. I was emotionally very connected to what was happening. Awareness of my recent concerns about my financial security came to mind, and I knew this was part of the chakra event taking place. I was also feeling relief that Dahli Lama would soon be experiencing security and companionship in her new life at the farm. After staying like that for a couple of minutes, she moved her buttocks around to the fence and had a good scratch after squaring up on it. Then she stopped scratching, moved her body all the way around and this time, placed her right side next to me, at her heart chakra area and stood there with me while I cried.

I never did see a single person on the ranch grounds the entire time I was there that day—and I was there for quite a while. I later learned that on the morning of my visit, an all-hands-on-deck rescue mission was underway at the far end of the ranch property. A mother and her newborn foal had somehow managed to become separated by a body of water. Happily, things turned out all right for baby and momma. And for the filly and me. Rescues all around.

I made arrangements for the young horse to be hauled over two days later, and I already had a name picked out for her. It had come to me during my drive back to Longmont with Maarten after our visit to Kesa Ranch.

Maarten began throwing out possible names for the filly. The name he was most enamored of was Dali, after Salvador

Dali. I smiled at that one, since Maarten was, among other things, a painter. I'd seen a few of his pieces, and they were definitely abstract in style. So it was probably natural for him to suggest naming such a lovely creature after one of the world's master artists.

I liked the name, but for a different reason: It conjured up a vision of the Dalai Lama.

"Oh my God," I said. "Do you realize that we both like the same name, but we have two different masters in mind? That's pretty crazy, right?"

Maarten laughed. To someone like me who had a love affair with words, this wordplay on Salvador Dali and the Dalai Lama was a thing of spontaneous beauty.

The idea of naming the filly with a nod to the enlightened Tibetan monk was appealing. Still, I didn't want her to have his *actual* name. I needed to make the name her own. Should it be Dalai, Dali, or something else? Dolly came to mind as well. But even though I knew little of the horse's personality at that point, Dolly seemed too saccharin for her. And then I had it: Dahli Lama!

The number of residents at the farm had grown quickly. In less than six months, our population had doubled. We began as a foursome: two cats, one dog, and one human. Then Cherokee and Saint came on board within hours of my arrival, followed by Stitch, a sweet male German Shepherd I adopted, and Dahli Lama. And we achieved perfect gender balance to boot.

It was remarkable to witness how calmly Dahli Lama stepped out of the trailer into her new Longmont surroundings— after her first trailer ride, no less. And when she took her place in the run on the other side of Cherokee's run, the equine duo became a trio without fuss or fanfare. She met her two elders with curiosity and respect, swiftly sizing up the herd dynamics and assuming her place within the hierarchy.

Heeding the counsel I was given, I kept Dahli Lama separated from Saint and Cherokee by a fence that divided two fields and kept a close watch on the horses. I was prepared to run out there if anything looked even slightly aggressive, although I had no idea how I would handle it if that did happen.

For much of the first day, Cherokee and Dahli Lama checked each other out along the fence line. Saint showed less interest in the newcomer and just grazed nearby. Peaceful relations prevailed throughout the day. I was elated when I caught sight of Dahli Lama and Cherokee grooming each other's backs. And though I'd been advised to keep the horses apart for at least a week, by the end of that first day, it seemed clear that wouldn't be necessary. Instead, I asked a horsewoman friend to come over the next day and be on hand when all three horses were released for the first time into a common space. Thankfully, that too went smoothly.

About four months after Dahli Lama's arrival, internationally respected animal communicator and foal gentler, Anna Twinney, came over and connected with all three horses. One of her first comments about the filly was, "She's unusually quiet and calm for a two-year- old."

During their communication, Dahli Lama conveyed to Anna that she wanted to show me what she could do, and when Anna asked her if she had any messages for me, Dahli

Lama's response was, "Be open to possibilities." I immediately asked Anna to tell Dahli Lama that I was definitely open.

And boy, as the days and weeks unfolded, Dahli Lama certainly did strutted her stuff and showed me what she could do. Her intelligence and spunk came out in many entertaining ways. About a month after her arrival, my ingenious young horse taught herself a stunt with her food bowl—and trained me to go along with it.

Besides keeping a plentiful supply of hay in each run, I also gave the horses bowls of grain for breakfast and dinner. At mealtimes, I kept them gated in their respective runs. This was largely because, on the one occasion I forgot to lock her in, Dahli Lama walked two runs over to Saint's run and consumed his remaining food. Being the submissive horse in the herd, Saint yielded his bowl to her without fuss. And although I promised Saint that I would never let that happen again, I did fail on two more occasions, for which I sincerely apologized.

The stunt happened while I was scooping poop in Cherokee's run one evening while he was finishing his dinner down at the other end. As usual, Dahli Lama had finished her meal ahead of both of her herdmates. I watched as she started nipping the edge of her bowl. After a few attempts, she got it lifted off the ground. It fell back down the first few times, but eventually, she managed to keep it between her teeth. Then she walked over to the rails separating her run from Cherokee's, and slipped the bowl in between the horizontal bars, right where I was standing! Flabbergasted, I quickly picked it up and walked over to Cherokee's bowl. I grabbed a handful of his grains, put them in Dahli Lama's bowl, and slid it back under the rails into her run.

Naturally, this positive reinforcement engendered a new ritual that has endured. After every meal, or whenever she spots an empty bowl on the ground, she picks it up. Then I say, "Bring me your bowl," and once I have it, I give her a few treats in exchange for the bowl. Then I quickly place the bowl out of sight.

Watching Dahli Lama become part of the herd was delightful. It was also reassuring to see my leadership skills improve as the weeks and months went by. I was learning how to set boundaries, tell her when she behaved in ways that weren't acceptable to me, and offer lots of praise for her acceptable behavior. One day a funny thought occurred to me: I had helped raise two daughters who had blossomed into highly confident, intelligent, and creative people. Two strong, young females making their way in the world. And now I had adopted a yearling who was already brimming with those same qualities as she, too, ventured into wider horizons. Another strong young female in my midst.

8

Herd Dynamics and Relationships

It wasn't hard to discern the particular habits, quirks, and preferences of each of the horses. Like humans, they had their likes and dislikes, preferences, and aversions. They posed questions and offered answers. And they felt and expressed uncertainty, confidence, hesitation, or courage depending on the situation and setting. In short, they were individuals.

On an admittedly superficial level, I took great delight in the fact that they each had their own distinct coloring and markings. Dahli Lama was a blue roan with a jet-black tail and mane, dark-grey coat tinged with indigo and silver tones, and a perfectly centered white diamond on her forehead. Saint was the redhead of the herd, with his orangey light-brown coat, a mane and a tail that each boasted multiple shades of blonde, and a long, irregularly shaped white blaze down the length of his face. And Cherokee sported a dark-bay coat, black mane and tail that each had coppery hints, and a small white "snip" asymmetrically located on the right side of his nose, down near his muzzle.

But it was another kind of variety in the herd, pointed out by my friend, Tamara, that took me by surprise, not only by what she shared but by the realization that I'd been oblivious to something so serendipitous—namely, their names. *Cherokee* had a Native American flavor to it, *Saint* was roughly Judeo-Christian, and *Dahli Lama* had a Buddhist/Eastern Mysticism quality to it. Having their names presented in this light really resonated for me. How had I missed that? Without any intentionality on my part, I had become the human guardian of a herd of horses with names hinting at spiritual pathways and traditions that, to greater or lesser extents, I had explored over the years.

On deeper levels, I noticed that the horses had distinct personalities and character traits. Thankfully, their individualities meshed together peacefully and allowed them to settle in comfortably with one another very quickly. Apart from that first day when Cherokee showed Saint, in no uncertain terms, who was in charge of run selection, they didn't seem to have any disputes or even mild disagreements to resolve. The same went for Dahli Lama in her relations with her mates. The three of them went about their interactions without incident. I didn't know if things flowed as smoothly as that every time horses were introduced to each other and asked to cohabitate, but I was grateful that it was flowing that way in my own herd.

Of course, it wouldn't have been enough for the horses to get along well among themselves. That same sense of ease needed to be present in *my* interactions with them as well. I also knew that I needed to be a leader they could always count on. As a novice, I felt blessed by how easy the horses made it for me to put my best foot forward and just keep going. Sometimes

I made mistakes and had to try hard to forgive myself. I suspected that the horses forgave me more quickly than I forgave myself each time.

One day I was out in the round pen with Cherokee on a late September evening. The flies were still out in full force, and I watched Cherokee's tail swatting them away. I decided to run back to the tack room and get the bottle of fly spray I'd forgotten to grab on my way out with Cherokee.

Back in the round pen, there was something else I forgot to do, which was show the bottle to Cherokee before starting to spray the repellent. Normally, I had a solid habit of showing the horses any objects that were going to be touching their bodies. But that evening, I forgot, and while standing close to the left side of Cherokee's neck, I raised the bottle and fired off the first spritz.

He immediately moved slightly back. No jolt, no bolt. Just a small but deliberate movement away from "the thing." Quickly realizing my misstep, I put the bottle down and offered my apology. As soon as I uttered the words, "I'm sorry. I'm so sorry. I promised you that you would have a voice. I'm sorry," Cherokee blinked quite emphatically. I had been taught that a single blink was one of the calming signals that horses (and other animals) sometimes used to convey, among other things, that they were fine and not feeling stressed. Cherokee's blink, coming as it did at that moment, was profound in its clarity of purpose.

I felt terrible about my faux pas but also knew it was important to return to the task and allow it to be carried out in a positive way. I stood with him another minute or so, softly stroking his neck, and then picked up the bottle. I held it up near his face. He blinked and I sprayed his whole body. All the while, he stood stock still, eyes soft, stance relaxed.

Everyone needs a voice.

I didn't do any real training with the horses until a few months after Dahli Lama joined the herd. Instead, the four of us spent those first several months getting acquainted with one another. All the while, I carried out my daily barn chores with deep contentment, gratitude, and clarity of purpose. As I moved from one task to the next, there was something so anchoring, so clean, about focusing my attention on each one.

There was also a sense of intimacy and sacredness to some caretaking duties in particular. Within a week of being hauled over to the property, Cherokee contracted an eye infection that required me to apply a ribbon of antibiotic ointment to his lower eyelid for several days. The first application required a lot of courage on my part and willingness on his. Fortunately, he submitted to my inexperienced but loving efforts without fuss, and together, we got the job done smoothly for the duration of the treatment.

Dahli Lama, too, developed a physical condition that needed my close attention. That caretaking, which was going to be on a long-term basis, also felt intimate and sacred. Rather than having been caused by an acute episode, as in Cherokee's case, Dahli Lama's difficulty arose from being toed-in on her front left leg. I had rescued and adopted her with the sole intention of partnering with her in my equine coaching business, not riding her, so she had never been ridden or even saddled. For the first year or so, she was fine.

But one day I noticed she was a little lame, and from then

on, our joined journey led us down new pathways. I took that development very hard and dedicated myself to finding out about the best ways to keep my girl pain free and sound. Surgery was not an option. Instead, I engaged a therapeutic farrier and made decisions about shoeing her front feet or leaving them unshod. I began experimenting with different treatment modalities, such as anti-inflammatory injections, CBD pellets, mineral supplements, infrared light therapy, and Reiki. I also prayed and listened to what my gut instincts told me. Each new discovery of a regimen that bore good results became the highlight of my day and my life.

Whether I was hanging out with the horses or ministering to physical conditions that arose, I respected their individuality and was willing to do whatever it took to earn and keep their trust. I related to the three of them as fellow travelers on the face of the earth, all of us journeying our way through our respective embodiments together. And with rare exceptions, our human-equine relations went smoothly.

Naturally, my emotional connection to each of them deepened with the passage of time, the amassing of shared experiences, and my ongoing education about horse care and horse mind. But even in the early going, I felt that the person I was in their company was the best version of myself. I couldn't help noticing that whenever I was in proximity to the herd (at least so long as I wasn't worried about any of them), my mind quieted, my shoulders dropped, and often, I would find myself suddenly taking a deep breath in and then out. I regularly felt waves of emotion that filled my eyes with tears. And it made little difference whether I was standing near them or some distance away. The sight of them grazing in a field, chewing hay in their runs, or standing still with a hind leg cocked as they gazed off into the distance brought feelings of peace, gratitude, and certainty that I was where I was meant to be.

It wasn't surprising to me–when I learned that there was a wealth of empirical and anecdotal findings to support the claim that being in the company of horses affected a person not just emotionally, but physiologically as well. It was believed that the heart, circulatory, respiratory, and neurological systems all benefited from the interaction with horses. My own experiences with Saint, Dahli Lama, and Cherokee certainly bore that out. When I was with them, either individually or as a group, I was affected emotionally, physically, and spiritually. And while I related to us as a close-knit family unit, the horses also showed me their individual personalities.

Saint was very laid back, not prone to emotional outbursts and content to be the submissive of the herd. Dahli Lama, while quite the confident creature, was nevertheless the youngster of the herd and knew instinctively that Cherokee was the horse in charge. Cherokee's role in the herd was that of leader, albeit a "passive leader," to use Mark Rashid's term for it. That is, he assumed and maintained his role with little fuss, which helped both Saint and Dahli Lama feel secure and free of stress.

In many ways, the day Elizabeth and I witnessed how the herd dynamics and hierarchy between Cherokee and Saint were established was one of my earliest schooldays in my equine education. As time went on, I noticed that horses were extremely efficient in the use of their energy. They didn't spend time or energy complicating situations with overthinking or self-criticism. Inwardly and outwardly, they were by nature peaceable creatures. It was no wonder that I derived such intense satisfaction from being in their company.

Before Dahli Lama came along, Cherokee and Saint grazed in tandem a good deal of the time, standing fairly close together. Once the dyad became a triad, Cherokee and Dahli Lama often grazed together, with Saint off by himself nearby. At first, this seemed like a lamentable development, something for which I projected pity onto Saint. But as the weeks and months passed, my anthropomorphic perspective loosened up. The more I trusted that my horses knew way more about being horses than I did, the more my human motherly distress fell away. What also helped was my observation of moments of true camaraderie between Saint and Dahli Lama.

For example, one day I was down at the barn watching the herd eat their dinner. After Cherokee and Dahli Lama were finished, Saint was still at it. My routine was to give all three horses their bowls, leaving Cherokee's and Dahli Lama's gates open but closing Saint's gate. Then I went back to the house and returned to the barn about twenty minutes later to open Saint's gate. He was not only the slowest eater of the herd, but according to the vet, he only had about half of his teeth, and of those, some were pretty worn down. So he wasn't even gaining the full benefit of the hay he consumed. If I didn't close him in, Dahli Lama would strut over to Saint's run and help herself to his remaining portion, feisty creature that she was.

That particular evening, I had already made my return trip to the barn to open Saint's gate. He was still eating, though, so I watched and waited. While I was there, a repairman arrived to inspect some water damage on the living room ceiling. Leaving Saint gated in, I hurried up to the house to greet the man, fully intending just to introduce myself, invite him into the house, and then return to Saint. Instead, we got to talking and I forgot all about my slow muncher.

As soon as I realized my lapse, I sprinted down to the barn, jumped over the fence, and approached Saint's run. There he was, at the gated end of the run, not making a sound. There was no whinnying to his herdmates to discover their whereabouts as he would normally do when unintentionally separated from them. Whenever that happened, I would run in the direction of whichever pasture his mates were in, yelling "Woo hoo, we're here, we're here" until Saint caught up to me and strode past me to join his mates. But this time, he stood there silently watching me.

For a few moments, I was stumped. But then, out of the corner of my eye, I spotted the reason for his lack of agitation. Dahli Lama was standing at the end of Cherokee's run, quietly looking over at me. I was astonished to see her there since Cherokee was gone and the gate to his run was wide open. She had chosen to hang back with her still-imprisoned herdmate, restraining herself from doing what she would otherwise have done, which was follow Cherokee out to the pasture.

I opened Saint's gate and watched him exit at his characteristically stoic walking gait. Dahli Lama immediately left Cherokee's run with a spryness in keeping with her youthfulness and spirited personality. Both of them spotted and joined Cherokee, who had chosen not to venture too deeply into the pasture without his mates.

Even with such beautiful camaraderie, the hierarchy was always present. When an intense heat wave descended and stuck around for several days, I kept a big bucket of water out in one of the fields, just to save the horses from having to walk the extra distance back to their stock tank. One day, I saw Dahli Lama walk over to the bucket and begin to slurp. A minute later, Saint came over and lowered his big head into the bucket. What a sight it was, the two of them sharing a watering hole, somehow managing to get their muzzles in there together. After a few moments, my enchantment with the collegial scene was shattered as Saint butted Dahli Lama's diamond-studded head right out of the bucket. Gone, gone, my sentimental reverie. That bubble had burst.

And it didn't end there. The next day, I spotted Saint sucking down water from that same bucket and then saw Cherokee come along and promptly butt *him* out of the way.

Herd dynamics and relationships at work. Or in this instance, it could be said that one comeuppance deserves another.

9

Rituals

Horses instinctively seek out security and equilibrium in their surroundings. They do need food, water, shelter, the companionship of other horses, and (if living with humans) positive interactions with humans. But in addition to these necessities, rituals can also be of great benefit to horses and their caretakers. Most of the rituals I've shared with my horses have arisen organically, from the heart.

One of our earliest rituals evolved on the first day I released Cherokee and Saint to one of the large fields. For the first few days, I had confined them to the corral around the barn so I could observe them more readily and familiarize myself with their normal behaviors, interactions, and habits. After that brief period, I felt confident about expanding their horizons, and for some reason, I chose the east pasture.

So after they finished their breakfast that morning, I opened the gates of their runs and began walking around the back of the barn. Both horses followed me, with Saint allowing Cherokee to go ahead of him. Instead of leading the three of us directly over to the east pasture gate, a fairly short distance away, I turned sharply to the right, which caused the three of us to cut a wide horseshoe-shaped circle around the inside perimeter of the corral. When we reached the gate, Saint and Cherokee stood quietly while I undid the latch and swung open the rail. I gave them each a cookie and then moved out of their way. And out they went.

As they traversed the long lane leading to the pasture, I watched their swishing tails and rounded rumps recede from view, disappearing altogether behind a stand of trees as the lane curved to the right and opened onto the field. I was mesmerized, enchanted, and deeply humbled. For several weeks, we circled around like that each morning. Then I changed our releasing ritual a bit and started releasing the horses to the west pasture as well. And once Dahli Lama came on board, those routines morphed yet again.

Sometime later, I learned that there was a term for what the three of us had been doing as we made our way over to the east pasture gate. Saint and Cherokee had been "walking at liberty" with me, a skill set that horses sometimes have to be trained to do. The naïveté I had brought to the activity that first time was probably what enticed the horses to circle around with me like that. My energetic field had been devoid of any mental chatter about whether or not they would obey, simply because it hadn't occurred to me that they wouldn't. I had innocently assumed that once I started walking, they would follow me. And so they did.

Of course, not all rituals endured. Some naturally fell away when circumstances changed or new needs arose. And some of them never took hold to begin with, leaving me to shrug my shoulders and surrender the idea. That was what happened on the day I tried to offer them a concert.

One chilly day shortly after moving in, I decided to bundle up and take my guitar out to the barn, thinking I might serenade Saint and Cherokee with a few songs. If things went as planned, I would treat them to a couple of covers and one or two of my originals. For sure, I wanted to play them, "The Story in Your Eyes," my favorite song by the Moody Blues. I was wide open to possibilities and happy to be trying something new with my beloveds.

Timing my arrival to coincide with their morning meal, I perched myself on a large overturned white bucket in a corner fifteen feet or so from the gated end of Saint's run. As I was setting up for the gig, both horses were still eating at the other end of their runs, so they had their backs to me.

I strummed my way through the introductory chords and started singing. About halfway through the first verse, Cherokee and Saint started making their way down to my end of their runs. As they neared their open gates, they stopped. I kept playing while we all eyed each other. Once those brief moments had passed, they promptly exited their runs and headed toward the west pasture gate.

Alas, a ritual in the making had been struck down at its premiere. No interspecies folk-rock band was going to be possible. I could have tied jangly bracelets around Cherokee's pasterns and taught him to step in time to the beat and maybe fastened a bell to the top rail of Saint's run and trained him to nudge it on cue with his generous muzzle. Then again, Cherokee probably would have resolutely refused to have jangly bracelets or any other musical instruments affixed to his body. And Saint would likely have not expressed any interest in the bell.

As I watched Saint and Cherokee walk out on the concert without so much as a glance in my direction, I couldn't help but grin. It *was* pretty funny. My audience of two was winnowed to zero before the end of the first verse. Was that their joint assessment of my abilities as a singer and guitarist? Maybe they would have preferred something in the jazz or classical vein.

Happily, some rituals did stick. For instance, bedtime prayers with the horses became my favorite ritual and favorite part of the day. Each evening, while the horses and I stand together in an intimate huddle, I am nourished by a strong sense of grounding, of knowing that I am exactly where I am supposed to be. I am so grateful that I get to give love in this prayerful way.

Without any bidding from me, Dahli Lama almost always takes one or two small steps back as soon as I say, "Okay, let's say prayers." I close my eyes, inhale and exhale, and bring my hands together before my heart. The horses keep their heads right up next to mine the whole time, even though there is plenty of fresh hay at our feet. While it's true that they know they'll be getting apple, carrot, or pellet treats once their person stops talking, I'm also certain that they respect and value this sacred time we share each day.

A set group of prayers naturally evolved. Some are recited in English and others in Sanskrit or Japanese. Some are accompanied by mudras and others by arm movements. I sound them in this order:

Om paramatmane namah. Ata.
(To the Supreme Atman, a bow.)
Safe passage through the night.
Good eyes, good guts, good extremities. Amen.
Om Tat Sat.
(Supreme Being, Brahman: That Thou Art.)
Thank you, God, for these great beings, great souls, great
teachers, great friends, great family. Amen.
Prayer time ends by chanting the three
Reiki Power Symbols, followed by:
Om. Shanti, Shanti, Shanti.
(Peace, Peace, Peace.)

After this, I give the horses a handful of kibble, apple, or carrot chunks while telling them to take good care of each other. Then I head over to the corral gate a short distance away. Sometimes the horses follow me out there, and when they do, I offer them a few more treats through the rails. Then I brush my hands together in front of my chest, say, "No more," and walk back to the house while making the same hand motions with my back to the horses.

One evening some time ago, I reached the front door of the house after prayers and glanced back at the barn. I noticed that Dahli Lama hadn't walked back inside. She was still standing next to the corral gate, looking directly at me. It felt like a moment to walk back and share a special moment with my girl. After giving her one more treat and a stroke down her nose, I wished her a good night and turned to leave. And that time, my arms instinctively shot up high above my head. With my hands slapping together up there, I headed back toward the house.

After walking several feet away, I stopped and looked back to confirm that she'd understood the meaning of these new gestures. Sure enough, she was already approaching the barn entrance. Clearly, she had understood my message: *I'm not coming back over there again. There will be no more treats.* And I understood hers: *I see. You're not coming back to give me more treats. There is no reason for me to stay here any longer.*

Since then and without fail, Dahli Lama stays out at the gate for as long as it takes, waiting for me to come back over. She stands there expectantly, with quiet confidence that I will play my part nicely. And so I do, ever since that first evening when we cocreated this sweet additional ritual. This is the one that's just between us gals.

10

Lessons from My Herd

To say that I stepped into my role as human guardian of a herd of horses with "beginner's mind" would be an understatement. I had everything to learn and none of it to take for granted. Some of the earliest lessons Dahli Lama, Saint, and Cherokee taught me came in serene moments, while others came about under dramatic circumstances. I was grateful for every lesson I learned and every message I received, for each one served to make me a better caretaker for my precious equine relatives.

One of the most important lessons I've learned from my herd is the importance of assessing whether or not a given situation or set of circumstances is truly a cause for panic or even concern. I noticed that whenever they had a strong reaction to something in their environment—some misstep on my part, perhaps, or some unfamiliar and disconcerting sound—once they determined that there was no imminent danger or cause for concern, they simply placed their attention back on whatever it was they'd been doing. This aspect of horse mind—which I've heard described as *What? Now what? So what?*—

was a kind of wisdom that I could sometimes emulate. . .and
sometimes not.

I've had a number of what I would call "first panic, then
peace" episodes with the herd. On those occasions, my fear for
the physical well-being of one or more of the horses is always
accompanied by concern for their emotional and mental states.

I needed to head down to Denver extra early one blustery
day, so I left the herd with what I hoped would be sufficient
quantities of hay to last them some eleven hours. I also made
sure the heating unit in their stock tank was working, given that
I was leaving the herd in the grips of nine frigid degrees. But
even before I hit southbound I-25, I began to have my doubts.
What if they ran out of hay before I was back? The mental image of the three of them burrowing their snouts several inches
down into the snow for hours in search of the meager winter
greens was distressing. Saint was a bit of a hard keeper, prone to
dropping weight, and this made me even more worried.

When my workday was over, I hurried home as fast as traffic and weather would allow. As I pulled up my long, snow-cov-
ered driveway, I prayed that none of the horses were suffering
an episode of colic. Prayers turned to pleas as I trudged through
the snow-buried path to the barn as quickly as my thick Car-
hartt overalls, chunky boots, heavy mash bucket, and the biting
wind would allow.

From some distance away, I was able to make out the shape
of Saint standing in his run. Clearly, he was alive and well. No
signs of distress. Then I spotted Cherokee standing in his own
run next to Saint's. He too was fine. But Dahli Lama was nowhere in sight. From what I could make out as I approached

the barn, her run was empty. Was she tucked way back at the far end of it, her body hidden in the shadows?

I reached the tack room, put the bucket down, and walked out to the runs to gain a closer look. For what must have been a mere five seconds or so, I still couldn't spot Dahli Lama. As anyone knows who has ever lost sight of a young child in public for that long, eternity becomes a relative term. So much turmoil was squeezed into those seconds. My heart thumped and my stomach knotted up as I frantically scanned the darkness. I pleaded, prayed, and promised never to complain about anything ever again, if only Dahli Lama was okay—all within that brief span of time.

Then I spotted her. She had been ridiculously and wonderfully close by the whole time, safe and sound in her run. Her dark-grey body and near-black head had simply been obscured from view. And like her herdmates, she was doing exactly what she was supposed to be doing at that hour—taking up her rightful position in preparation for the imminent arrival of Meal Ticket Mom.

Relieved that the horses all seemed fine, I was able to calm down and watch them contentedly eat their dinner. I noticed my heartbeats slowing, and it occurred to me that maybe some of that ancient equine wisdom was rubbing off on me.

Sometimes my sense of imminent danger was triggered by little more than my lack of experience. One evening while I was still a student in the TBAH coaching program, I was invited out to a group dinner with several other students. We were meeting at La Mariposa, a Mexican restaurant in nearby Lyons. Kim, my good friend from the program, pulled into the parking lot at the same time as me, so we walked in together and ordered margaritas. A few of the other students were there as well, but nearly an hour later, we were still several folks shy of the whole group. By then I was pretty miffed. I was also agitated at the prospect of getting home to the herd much later than I'd intended. But since Melisa was among the missing, nobody wanted to start placing their dinner orders.

Finally, it became excruciating to continue making small talk, so I stood up and announced to a startled Kim that I was leaving. I told her that I needed to make my escape before the delayed festivities really got underway. I had no cash and didn't want to stick around long enough to flag down a waitress, hand her my plastic, and then wait for the processing to be completed. So I asked Kim to please pay for my drink, then I kissed her and hurried out to the parking lot. I felt an urgent need to get home.

When I got there, I spotted the horses at the far end of the field surrounding the barn. What I saw was something that was either wonderful or horrendous. In the dimming light of the dusky hour, I couldn't tell which and stood there transfixed, staring at them.

Cherokee was down. He was lying on his side with his head down rather than in a half-sitting position with his legs tucked under him. Dahli Lama and Saint stood off to the side. I'd never seen horses lying down like that—except maybe in movies, after they'd been shot.

Was he dead or was he just hanging out with his buddies, taking in the pleasant coolness of the evening? On the one hand, I couldn't wait to get closer so I could marvel at the sight of my horse in such a deeply relaxed posture. But on the other hand, the thought that I might be coming face-to-face with a dead horse—my horse—was paralyzing.

I knew I had to get a move on, but I felt immobilized. My first step was accompanied by a deep intake of air. I hadn't realized I'd been holding my breath all that time. I walked slowly and silently across the field, resisting the urge to run in case everything was copesetic. But if Cherokee *was* in acute distress, there was no time to lose. I kept my eyes trained on him as I advanced. My brain did at least register that he wasn't frantically rolling around, which would have been a definite sign of trouble. That, I knew, was a good thing. But since what I feared was something even worse than colic, I wasn't able to take much comfort in that as I approached.

When I was within several yards of the fence that separated me from the horses, Saint turned his head and looked over at me. That had the effect of alerting Cherokee, who then moved his head ever so slightly. He moved! Seeing that he was alive, I felt the dread immediately drain from my head down to my feet, where the earth magnanimously received all five hundred tons of it.

I could have crawled under the fence then to approach the horses and stroke their noses once or twice. But I chose not to, despite how glorious an experience it would have been. That Cherokee was alive and well was glory enough for me, and the last thing I wanted to do was disturb the equine tranquility.

Panic had given way to peace. As I walked back to the house, I could hear my dogs, Billy and Stitch, barking their greetings. And now, with no fear to freeze my footfalls, I quickened my gait.

But not all of the lessons from my herd have been about

returning to peace after a real or imaginary threat has been re-
solved. Some have been about trust—trust in my ability to do
the right thing for my horses (as well as my other animal relatives) and trust in my relationships with all of them.

Early one sunny morning I was awakened by the sound of
Beto's voice calling my name. He was a ranch hand who worked
on my landlord's property, farther down Journey Lane, and he
also came over from time to time to make repairs to things in or
around my farmhouse. Beto was always in good cheer, but right
then his voice sounded anything but cheerful. He was yelling to
me from his truck that Cherokee and Dahli Lama were up on the
mountainside, about a quarter mile to the west of the farmhouse.
Blessedly, Saint had stayed back on the farmhouse grounds.

Half asleep, I threw on a sweatshirt, raced down to the
barn, filled both pockets with the highest value treats I had on
hand, and grabbed two halters and leads. On the way back to
Beto's truck, I noticed the gate on the fence that separated my
property from my landlord's was open. (I found out later that a
ranch hand had come onto my property to carry out a mainte-
nance task and left that gate open when he was done.) That had
allowed Cherokee and Dahli Lama to get loose and make their
way over to Rabbit Mountain by traversing my landlord's huge
unenclosed field.

For the moment, the horses were within sight, grazing on
the upward slope of the mountain. But there were no fences or
other barriers to keep them from either traveling deeper into
the mountains or accessing the road that was less than a mile
away. I climbed into Beto's truck, and we drove a little farther
down Journey Lane before cutting diagonally across the un-

fenced field. Though I was struggling to process that this was actually happening, I was alert enough to feel panic creeping in.

When we were still quite a ways shy of where the mountainside slope began, I was about to tell Beto to stop the truck and let me out because I knew the horses were less likely to bolt if they saw a person approaching instead of a loud truck. But then I noticed that Randy, another of my landlord's ranch hands, was also driving across the field from a different direction. He was actually pulling ahead of us, aiming his truck directly toward the two distant horses. That was definitely not what I wanted.

Sure enough, alerted to what was happening, the horses moved farther up the side of the mountain. Great. Now what? Beto brought his truck to a stop. I didn't want to shout across the distance to Randy, so I asked Beto to call him and tell him to get the hell out of there. That worked. Randy turned his truck around and headed back in the direction of the farmhouse. Still, I now had an even greater distance to cover on foot, thanks to the horses having been spooked.

While maintaining a laser-like focus on the task at hand, I was also fending off a raw combination of disbelief, barely checked panic, and a desire to dissociate from a situation that had the potential for unmitigated disaster. I was also aware that I was due at work later that morning.

But apart from the inner turmoil, there was something else coursing through my veins: trust. Trust that the connection I shared with Dahli Lama and Cherokee would prove strong enough to keep them from running away and trust in the knowingness that it was all going to turn out all right.

I began walking up the slope toward the horses, keeping my energy low and calm and my pace slow and relaxed. I was keenly aware that I wasn't going to get anywhere near either of them unless they each made the decision to allow that. We were in the great wide open where *their* wishes ruled supreme.

As I drew closer, I could see that they were grazing several feet away from one another. Dahli Lama was closest to me and spotted me first. Soon enough, though, Cherokee also raised his head in my direction. I immediately dropped my gaze and took a few steps back.

Approach and release was one of the key techniques I'd learned for building strong relationships with my horses. I had used that technique successfully with the herd on many occasions when I needed to approach them in one of the large pastures to halter and bring them back down to the barn. I would walk toward them (the approach) and then stop at intervals to turn a shoulder to them and look down at the ground (the release). And then I would resume my approach. Timing was critical, but sometimes my timing was off and I didn't release the pressure soon enough—or the horses just didn't want to be caught. Either way, the worst thing that had ever happened was that the horses walked or ran away from me within those blessedly enclosed spaces.

But that morning, the stakes were much higher, and I needed to get it right. After gazing at the ground for several seconds, I looked up again and saw that both horses had resumed their grazing. They had noticed me and were unconcerned enough to resume grazing, which meant that they were viewing me as a nonthreatening herd member. As I made my approach, Dahli

Lama and Cherokee occasionally raised their heads and looked in my direction. When that happened, I stopped walking, turned my body to the side, and stared off into space or down at the ground. A few times, I bent down and brushed the grass with a hand. Then I began walking again. All those behaviors were meant to show the horses (prey animals) that I (a human and therefore a predator) was not a danger to them, that I meant them no harm, and that they were safe to keep doing whatever they were doing

Finally, I was close enough to the horses to implement the next part of my plan. With my left shoulder turned toward Dahli Lama, I reached into my left coat pocket for a generous handful of treats and then extended my arm toward her. In my right hand, I held a halter with a lead attached to it. Gazing downward, I envisioned the specific actions I would take if she came over to investigate. Out of the corner of my eye, I saw her looking at me. Then she started walking down the slope toward me. As soon as I felt her muzzle nibbling from my left hand, I turned toward her, raised my right arm, and slowly draped the halter and lead around her neck. Then, after reaching under her jaw to take hold of both ends, I drew out another big handful of treats from my pocket. While she was occupied with the kibble, I somehow managed to finagle the dangling halter into place on her head.

The second halter and lead were still draped over my left arm, and Cherokee was a short distance away. I felt confident that once he noticed me walking away with his herdmate, he would catch up to us and I could repeat the procedure I'd used with Dahli Lama. Before Dahli Lama and I had gone very far, I saw that Cherokee had already turned himself around and was heading toward us. When he caught up to us, I sensed that I needed to keep walking and not stop to halter or secure him in any way. That was another knowingness I chose to trust.

As we came down the slope and stepped onto the huge field we would need to cross, I remembered to look straight ahead, adhering to the principle I'd been taught that you should look in the direction you want your horse to go. Thankfully, the horses did nothing to concern or alarm me. But while it was a blessedly calm procession, it was also more than a little surreal.

Finally, I saw the fence that surrounded my side yard, just a few hundred feet ahead of us. I let my eyes search out the twelve-foot gate attached to it, but then I remembered to return to looking straight ahead. When we had nearly reached Journey Lane, I caught sight of Randy's truck about fifty feet beyond the gate. Apprehension seized me. If he got out of his truck to help or even just shouted over to me, there was a real possibility that the horses might spook and take off, especially Cherokee.

When we reached the gate, I unlatched it with my free hand. Once we were safely inside, I removed Dahli Lama's halter and watched her catch up to Cherokee, who was already racing across the yard. As for me, if I hustled, I could still make it to work on time.

It had been a joined journey of a sort I hoped never to take again with any of my horses. Still, over the next few days, as I reflected on the experience, I felt thankful for more than the happy ending. I was also grateful for the lesson learned about the power of trust. I recognized that throughout the whole ordeal, there had been several kinds of trust at work: trust in my relationship with the horses, trust in Cherokee's and Dahli La-ma's willingness to submit to my leadership instead of fleeing it, trust in the sense I had at the outset with the message that it was all going to be all right, and trust in the knowledge that kept presenting itself and guiding my actions.

That wasn't my first mountainside experience with Chero-kee in which trust had played a huge part. A few months after moving to the farm, I rode him up along a section of Rabbit Mountain that sat about five hundred feet beyond the western-most border of the farmhouse property. I was accompanied by three new acquaintances, all of them much more seasoned rid-ers than me. We maintained a leisurely pace, traveling along a hogback with a gradual slope that opened onto a large partially fenced clearing.

We stopped there to take in the gorgeous panoramic views. After a minute or so, Cherokee started walking the two of us off toward an unfenced area. Within seconds, he moved up from a walk to a trot and then, before I knew it, to a spirited canter. I was stunned by how quickly we'd arrived at the edge of what looked, at least to me, like a very steep downward slope. I panicked.

Because I panicked, I didn't do any number of things I could have done to get Cherokee to turn to his left, turn to his right, or come to a full stop. I knew what was supposed to be done with my reins, my arms, my hands, and my hips, but I didn't do any of those things. And there was one more thing I didn't do. I didn't go for it and take the ride down the mountainside.

It might have been a special shared experience, exhilarating and confidence-building—assuming, of course, that I'd stayed put in the saddle. Cherokee and I will never know how that equine sleigh ride might have gone. The truth is, my lack of control or lucidity was as stunning as the speed with which we'd arrived at the precipice.

My biggest misstep that day was to panic. My hands and arms shot way up high, away from my body, rather than remaining low and tucked into my hips. And I screamed. I screamed and bailed off Cherokee, rolling slightly down the slope. Luckily, I came away with only a few scratches on my face and one arm. I got up, found my glasses nearby, and cleaned myself off.

While grateful that I was safe, I immediately plunged into a new panic mode. Where was Cherokee? What if he was alarmed and had bolted? What if he was gone for good? I scanned the clearing and quickly spotted him. Bless his heart, he hadn't run away. He was standing several feet away from the other three horses, whose mounts were all taking in the unfolding drama. Perhaps his instinct had been to rejoin the other members of his species rather than run off alone into wholly unknown territory.

The other riders were discussing how best to capture Cherokee. Their plan was to back him into the fenced area of the clearing and then surround him. They succeeded in getting him to move slightly backward. But he also moved to his left, which bridged some of the distance between us. Even though he could easily have escaped, he chose instead to come to a stop about fifteen feet away from me.

As Cherokee and I stood there looking at one another, I knew that I alone was going to approach him. My intuition told me that he would respond much better to my energy, my intention, and my love. Trusting in that knowledge and in our deep relationship, I told everyone in a quiet but firm voice that I was going to get my horse by myself. One of the other riders resisted for a moment but relented when I repeated myself while at the same time maintaining eye contact with Cherokee.

I took a few moments to become still and then began walking slowly toward Cherokee in increments of a foot or so, pausing in between each advance. When I reached him, he stayed put as I slowly reached up and took hold of his bridle with my left hand. With my other hand, I stroked his neck and thanked him for not running away. One of the men came over to help me mount up and muttered an unkind comment about how one should never bail from a horse.

That evening, I took a leisurely bubble bath and reflected on the day's misadventure. First, I used my cell phone to search the internet for articles about bailing from a horse. I took great solace in discovering that many seasoned horsemen consider it to be an acceptable choice in certain situations. After that, I closed my eyes and tried to envision my perfect execution of a couple of the techniques. As I did so, I realized that given my inexperience with those maneuvers and my panicked state, there was a good chance I might have executed them poorly enough to have caused a much worse outcome for Cherokee and me.

I knew I needed to put speculation to rest and forgive myself for not having been able to do things differently with Cherokee. I reminded myself that we were both safe and sound. I added more hot water to the bath, and with my eyes still closed, I pictured Cherokee and me facing each other up there on the clearing in the moments before I approached him.

Holding this image in mind and heart allowed me to have the best realization of my hours-long soak: It wasn't that I had succeeded in capturing Cherokee. It was that he had chosen to let himself be rescued by me. He had counted on his person to get him out of that stressful situation, and our bond was deep and sure-footed enough for that to happen. Our safekeeping that day was down to one thing alone: the trust that we had both instinctively placed in one another and in our connection.

In living with my equine relatives, I have learned a wealth of lessons about how to serve their highest welfare, as well as my own. I am grateful for every lesson learned and every message received, whatever it is about: trust; patience; forgiveness; the need to be congruent in thought, word, and action; or the benefits of having a sense of humor. One of the most impactful lessons I've learned from the herd is that peacefulness is the default state for horses. That is their true north, their energetic home. I do my best to integrate that lesson into my daily life. It's not always easy, but my horses have been setting fine examples for me for years. They're pros at it.

Author with Cherokee

Left to Right: Dahli Lama, Saint, Cherokee

11

Lessons from My Trainer

From the get-go, I had a simple—some might say naïve—confidence that my deep love for the horses would be a portal for knowledge to flow through about how best to care for them. With time, experience, and that open portal, trust in my capacity to discern what the horses needed in a given situation continued to deepen.

Still, I was truly a neophyte when it came to horse care. I followed my instincts, which told me to limit the number of horse experts who would have influence over my decisions or who would have interactions with the herd. I didn't want the joined journey the four of us were embarking upon to be flooded with a barrage of information from too many sources, well-meaning though they might have been. Our circle of influencers was kept small and intimate.

For the better part of the first year, I mostly handled the herd's welfare by trying to follow the Hippocratic Oath: First do no harm. I provided the horses with good quality hay, decent grains, fresh water, and lots of time to hang out together in the farm paddocks and fields. I decided to keep the horses barefoot and engaged a wonderful trimmer.

Eventually, I felt a desire to start taking riding lessons. During the Women's Quest retreat, I had neither trouble nor fear riding Cherokee at various gaits, including a surprise gallop on two occasions. I trusted Cherokee, and he kept me safe from start to finish. Still, I knew I needed some formal training. I'd never had horseback riding lessons, and while I recognized that I didn't know a whole heck of a lot, I had no sense of the *scope* of the void.

But my naïveté extended beyond that to something of a different nature. I had never, even for a moment, contemplated that Cherokee and I wouldn't simply pick up where we'd left off. He'd made it look and feel so easy at the retreat. As it turned out—this was my theory, anyway—the combination of his being freed up from the life of a dude ranch horse coupled with my limited experience with anything other than nose to tail trail riding proved a bit challenging.

Fortunately, my friend, Kim, not only recommended trainer Bill Pelkey, she was insistent about it. "You need to call Bill, Nancy. He's going to be a perfect fit for you and your horses. Call him!"

I made the call and Bill came over a couple of days later, on his birthday, no less. From a distance, he watched me interact with Cherokee for a while then commented, "Yep, he's your horse all right." He spent some time with all three horses while sharing his approach to horsemanship and life itself. He was, indeed, a great fit: friendly, knowledgeable, clearly intent on treating horses with respect, free of any sense of superiority over horses—and metaphysically inclined to boot.

Bill quickly became one of our most important influencers, and he helped the horses and me achieve a life of harmony, mutual respect, and love. Bill articulated and demonstrated principles of caretaking, groundwork, and riding in ways that I was able to grasp and apply, sometimes with ease and other times after considerable practice. He also pointed out the many subtle ways we humans unintentionally and often unconsciously convey messages to horses with our body language, emotional and mental states, and unspoken agendas. His trove of knowledge about horse mind and human mind helped shape me into the kind of human guardian and companion I wanted to be for my horses.

An example of Bill's caretaking came as a result of some less than acceptable behavior from Dahli Lama. One day, Dahli Lama decided to send a territorial message to my dog, Billy. She kicked out one of her hind legs in his direction, barely missing him. For weeks afterward, my otherwise happy-go-lucky boy did not trust Dahli Lama and steered clear of the runs entirely.

I had an experience of my own with her that involved nipping rather than kicking. And afterward, like Billy, I cycled through a period of trusting, distrusting, and then renewing trust in Dahli Lama. But *unlike* Billy, I needed more than just a few weeks to complete that circuit.

When I adopted Dahli Lama, she expressed absolutely no concerns about my touching or handling any area of her body. She exuded calmness and confidence, which inspired the same in me. I got used to this ease of being with her, and I naïvely thought the trajectory of our relationship would continue flowing in an unerringly positive arc with no challenges to overcome or fears to conquer.

But one day when she was about a year and a half, something happened that caused me to have serious doubts about that arc. I was standing next to Dahli Lama in her run when she snapped her head around and nipped me in the arm. I was stunned and flat-out shocked. To my still inexperienced eye, her behavior seemed unwarranted, sudden, and without warning. More likely, I had missed the cues.

After it happened, I didn't do anything to reassert my authority. Not only had I not yet learned *that* particular skill set, I wasn't even aware of the need for it. Instead, I walked away from her, rubbing my arm as I headed back to the house. After that episode, I became hesitant to be in close physical proximity to Dahli Lama or interact with her in any intimate way. My apprehension about bodily harm was rendered exponentially worse by the accompanying emotional distress. It made me sad to find myself living in fear of one of my own. The result of sloshing around in this emotional soup was that some serious existential doubts began to creep in. Had I made a huge mistake in adopting her? Was I really up for this? Why was she doing this to me? Was it going to get even worse?

A few days after that nip, Bill arrived for my lesson with Cherokee. When we were done and I had released Cherokee from the round pen, I asked Bill if he had a few minutes to talk about Dahli Lama. No sooner had I begun speaking than the tears came. I told him what had happened and then blurted out, "Our relationship has to be rehabilitated, Bill."

Bill placed both hands on my shoulders and smiled. "Your

relationship doesn't need to be rehabilitated, Nancy. You just need to learn how to get big with that girl." His tone was kind and not the least bit condescending, though he categorically disagreed with my take on the situation. Instead of agreeing with my assessment, he expressed his confidence in my ability to work with Dahli Lama to resolve our issues. He explained that Dahli Lama was testing me, assessing my leadership chops. Her survival instincts compelled her to determine whether I was a reliable and consistent leader in whom she could place her trust.

Over the next few months, Bill gave me a crash course in how to "get big" with my girl when she was behaving disrespectfully or dangerously. In particular, he demonstrated two simple things I could do, both of which would remind her that, of the two of us, I was the "boss mare." The first was to take my index finger and tap firmly and repeatedly under one of her eyes while staring intently into it. The second possible response was to pinch the side of her lower lip between my thumb and one or two fingers for a few seconds while, again, holding her in my intent gaze.

At first, it wasn't easy for me to express dominance in either of those ways, but I knew I had to be a strong leader and take action. Although Dahli Lama had by now only landed two or three actual nips, she'd also made a few unsuccessful attempts. Clearly, my mare needed manners and I needed safety. So I dismissed any sentimentality and persevered. In fairly short order, the unwanted behavior was extinguished.

Shortly thereafter, though, we went through similar nipping episodes in a whole new setting: hoof picking time. One day while picking her left front hoof, I suddenly felt that familiar sharp pain on my left arm. She'd nipped me! I stood up and planted several quick taps under her left eye while staring at her and saying something or other to her in a sharp tone. I resumed my picking, albeit a bit nervously, and finished the task. But that stinker made a few more attempts to sneak in a nip the next few times I picked her hooves. Damn! Even though I was a bit more seasoned by then and much less fearful of my mare, it was still extremely annoying to be startled like that while concentrating so intently on the task at hand.

An idea came to mind. Before starting another picking session, I put a halter and lead on Dahli Lama and let the lead hang down to the ground. Every once in a while, I gave a little tug on the lead to remind her that I was keeping an eye on whether her head (and teeth) were still facing straight ahead. That turned out to be an effective and efficient solution. Soon enough, it was no longer needed, and we went back to halter-free hoof picking.

For several years, Bill came over and gave me lessons in what he referred to as the "Spanish Californio Nevada" tradition. But his eclectic skill set offered so much more than that: patience with my frequent ineptitudes; a multitude of tricks and techniques learned or created over his forty-odd years as a horseman; and a natural inclination to respect not merely the physical states and needs of the horses when he interacted with them, but their mental and emotional ones as well. Since I instinctively sought to care for each of those dimensions of my animal relatives, equine or otherwise, Bill was an ideal match for me. In essence, he was my personal treasure trove of knowledge, guidance, and encouragement.

Sometimes our groundwork or riding lesson would be cut short so Bill could do body or energy work with one or more of the horses. Whenever that happened, I never had a sense that I'd missed out on having a "real" lesson. On the contrary, I always counted my blessings that the horses and I were fortunate to have a trainer who was willing to see what needs arose in the moment and switched the agenda if needed.

Bill's respect for and kinship with Cherokee, Dahli Lama, and Saint were among his most precious gifts, along with his never-failing support of their human guardian. I called Bill countless times when I feared for the well-being of one or another of the horses, and more often than not, he drove the half hour or so from Loveland to see for himself what was happening. On those occasions when he couldn't come, he stayed on the phone with me, assessing the situation as best he could, based on my (sometimes panicked) descriptions.

He was always conscientious about telling me that since he was not a veterinarian, I should feel free to seek a medical consultation. If a vet did come out, Bill always tried his best to be there. I'm certain that this wasn't solely out of concern for the horse's distress but for mine as well. While the veterinarian was present, I was usually able to carry on without breaking down. As long as the news wasn't bad, that is. If the news *was* bad, it was very hard not to get weepy. I tried my best to cowgirl up, but once the doctor was gone, I usually broke into tears, either from worry or from the release of fear. Regardless of the outcome, it was always a great comfort to have Bill on hand to lend me emotional support during those farm calls.

Regarding training, I had absolutely no interest in methods

that involved domination or force. Instead, I did my caretaking, groundwork, and training in accordance with two principles that Bill had learned years earlier and passed on to me. Those principles allowed me to interact with my herd in ways that aligned with the lens through which I viewed them and our joined journey.

The first of those, *primus inter pares* (first among equals) was initially applied by Bill in the context of managerial positions he had held in various non-equine business ventures. Later on, he adopted this principle to his eclectic style of horse training. In essence, it meant encouraging the horse to feel a sense of partnership with the person while at the same time making sure that the horse respected the person as leader of the two. Egotistical superiority, no; benevolent leadership, yes.

The second principle, *solvitur en modo, firmitur en rey* (gentle in what you do, firm in how you do it) was said to be a favorite of internationally respected horseman, Buck Brannaman. For me, it meant asking for a certain behavior or response from my horse while employing nonaggressive techniques and remaining committed to the process all the way through, until he or she complied either fully or closely enough for me.

Cherokee, for instance, usually offered me the minimum he could get away with, not resentfully or begrudgingly—well, perhaps a bit begrudgingly at times. But since I'd shown him my acceptance of his modus operandi, right from the get-go, I couldn't complain. I had to play fair. So, if I asked him to move his foot back and he moved it an inch, that was compliance. If I then asked him to move it a little more and he moved it ever so slightly farther back, that too was compliance—coming from him.

Through spending time with my herd, I came to understand that horses conveyed their wants and needs, as well as likes and aversions, in clear-cut ways. They showed when they were either at ease or ill at ease. They didn't dissemble. They also didn't employ sarcasm, irony, or double entendre. They were masters of honesty and precision, and their messages weren't hard to miss once you'd been shown what to look for. For instance, when a horse pinned his or her ears flat back, it was best to avoid standing within striking distance of their long legs, solid jaw, or large teeth. And you definitely didn't want to be on the receiving end of a horse's irritated tail swish. It stung like hell.

One of Bill's finest pieces of advice was one I brought to mind often (and still do). I considered it to be a golden rule of thumb, a litmus test for gauging whether or not to worry about horses in inclement weather conditions, especially insofar as the dreaded colic was concerned. Without taking into account any health issues that a particular horse might have, it went like this: As long as horses were not exposed to a combination of cold, wind, and wet, there was little reason to fret. So on a day when high winds were blowing and the temperature had fallen to fifteen degrees Fahrenheit, so long as it was dry, the horses were likely to be just fine. Similarly, there was little cause for concern if it was raining with gusting winds, but the temperature was a balmy (for horses) forty degrees or if it was fifteen degrees outside with rain, but the air was still.

But if the wind was blowing up a storm, it was that same fifteen degrees out, and it was sleeting, that was a very troubling trifecta. In that scenario, the horses stayed in, with extra hay in their bins and the deicer in their stock tank. I also offered them extra grains between breakfast and dinner and walked out to the barn late at night, to make sure they seemed fine and hadn't gone through all of their hay.

Admittedly, I often checked on the horses anyway when it rained hard, even when there were no high winds or extremely low temperatures. Nine times out of ten, the horses had exercised the good sense to come in from the field and take shelter. But I always felt that getting myself drenched was well worth it, whether it turned out to be one of those nine occasions or the tenth one.

Over time, Bill's lesson in this regard, and in many others, helped me distinguish between what constituted a true emergency and what did not. Still, those priceless lessons didn't change who I was and still am: a softhearted animal lover to the core.

12

Lessons through Animal Communication

Soon after moving into the farmhouse, I began associating with and befriending folks who had serious chops in energy work that included somatic awareness, clairsentience, chakra alignment, Reiki, and interspecies telepathic communication. I was deeply intrigued and amazed, and I was keen to develop my own skills in those areas.

In my early forays into telepathic interspecies communication, I was sometimes dismayed about my nascent abilities and wondered if what I had just experienced had been telepathy or imagination. But I was told that this was typical for those with limited practice or experience with telepathy and that it was critical that I err on the side of trusting the messages I was getting because *acknowledging* them was essential for deepening the capacity to *receive* them.

So I developed the conscious habit of honoring my own experiences, regardless of how significant or trivial they felt and regardless of whether I was one hundred percent certain that the messages hadn't come from my imagination. The most valuable pieces of advice I received were that imagination didn't need to be eschewed when practicing telepathic communication with animals or humans and that self-criticism and second-guessing were hindrances to one's practice.

Even so, as I began developing those skills, there were times when it proved impossible for me to avoid self-criticism. That happened when I attended a weekend-long animal communication workshop in Elizabeth, Colorado, about two hours south of Longmont. In several one-on-one sessions, the ten of us practiced sending messages to and receiving messages from the birds, dogs, and horses present. We were encouraged to take note of whether we were experiencing words, somatic sensations, mental images, gut feelings, tears, or something else. While I did experience a couple of connections, they were superficial at best. To my mind and heart, I had failed to engage any of the creatures in what I considered in-depth communications.

The big finish came on Sunday afternoon with a session in remote viewing. We were paired off into five couples and received a brief set of instructions, and then we went to work. The object was to describe our partner's dwelling place or property in detail. My partner was armed solely with the knowledge that I lived in a house with two dogs, one of whom was white. After some time and encouragement from the workshop facilitator, who came by and briefly knelt down next to us, my partner was able to see the layout of both levels of my farmhouse, as well as the red barn on the property. As her closing salvo, she added, "And I see a dog running toward a barn, a red barn. And it's the white dog. He's the one who really loves going to the barn."

Ka-ching. She was right on the money. Of the two dogs, Billy *was* the one who absolutely loved hunting down tasty dung apples in the horse runs. (Stitch trotted along as well, but I knew it was largely because he wanted to be with Billy and me.) I was astonished by my partner's ability and accuracy. After we switched roles and I attempted to see *her* dwelling, astonishment turned to distress. Of *her* home and property, I saw nothing, inside or out. Eight out of ten of us were successful in seeing and describing their partner's dwelling in detail. I was not one of the lucky eight.

When it came time to head home, I was knotted up with distress. I gathered up my things and waited for the workshop leader to be surrounded by others so I could slip away unnoticed. I felt bad not saying good-bye or expressing my thanks, but I didn't want to engage in conversation with her about how the workshop had gone for me. I broke into a jog and made it to my car before anyone else even got to the parking area. The drive back to Longmont was unintentionally circuitous because I had distractedly traveled too far west, ending up in the foothills just outside Golden.

I opened the front door and lay down on the bare wooden floor. Both dogs were at my sides within minutes. Stitch's tongue glommed onto my right cheek and Billy's went to work on the other. Lying there with my arms pressed to my sides, I let them have their way with me, grateful for the frenzied healing. As they blessed me with kisses and licked away my salty tears, their joint message came through loud, clear, and wet: *We're so glad you're home!*

I had better luck at other times, both at keeping my ego

in check and in successfully communicating. One November evening, I got home late from the law office I was working at in Denver, greeted the dogs and cats, and prepared a big bucket of dinner grains for the horses. On the rare occasions when I got home later than usual, I sometimes found their runs empty when I got there to feed them. Whenever that happened, I felt pangs of guilt and had to shake off the image of the three of them forlornly giving up and abandoning their runs.

Sure enough, the horses were nowhere in sight. I put down the bucket of mash and headed over to the west pasture gate. I knew they wouldn't be in the east pasture since I had that gate closed. But when I saw that the western gate was also closed, I realized that strong winds must have blown it shut. Commissioning a large rock on the ground as a gate stop, I propped the gate open and stood just inside the pasture, alternating between making sounds to let the herd know I was there and silently letting the listening go wide. My herd was hidden somewhere out there, and I anxiously awaited the thundering sound of hooves closing the distance between us. But out there in the inky night, I heard only the usual buzzing, humming, and swishing sounds of nature. No hooves and no horses.

I kept up that pattern a few minutes and then remembered something Bill had told me many times: Horses hear us best through the silent channels of energetic fields and other nonverbal pathways. Fueled by that, I decided to experiment. I climbed onto a nearby split rail fence, perched on the top rail facing out toward the pasture, and adjusted myself to make certain that I felt securely balanced. I didn't want my attention focused on my body any more than necessary.

My intention was to call out to Cherokee silently and ask him to bring the herd in from the pasture. I closed my eyes and conjured in mind an image of Cherokee's chocolate-colored form. At first, I pictured him standing way back at the far end of the pasture. But I refreshed the image a few times, envisioning him either walking or running across the field toward me. All the while, I sounded in mind, *Cherokee, bring the herd down. Cherokee, bring the herd down. Cherokee, bring the herd down.*

I opened my eyes every now and then and listened out into the darkness, taking my time with the process and feeling neither agitated nor hurried. At some point, it occurred to me that I needed to be more precise and sounded in my mind, *Cherokee, bring the herd down to the barn for dinner.* A few times I sounded his name alone while holding his image in mind. I felt a certainty about my connection with Cherokee, and that absence of doubt was both grounding and liberating. I came away with an understanding that this certainty of connection was a form of interspecies communication, no less valid than any others.

Time passed, and when I finally opened my eyes, there he was. Cherokee was walking directly toward me through the darkness. He stopped about six feet away from me. I sat there transfixed and then reached into the right pocket of my jacket for a horse treat and offered it to him. But it was my last treat, and I took that as my cue to hop down, walk over to the gate, and see if Cherokee would follow me. He did, and I walked him back to his run.

Although it was curious to me that Cherokee had come down from the pasture alone—something I had never before seen him do—I took his arrival as confirmation that he *had* heard my requests. I figured I would just have to wait and see how the rest of the message about bringing Dahli Lama and Saint down was going to play out. For the moment, I needed to feed Cherokee.

While he was still eating, I remembered that I had left the pasture gate open, as well as the one at the end of Cherokee's run. I didn't want Cherokee to head back out to pasture before Dahli Lama and Saint came down to eat, since they were still missing. So I left Cherokee's run and headed toward the pasture gate. As I rounded the corner of the barn, there was Dahli Lama walking toward me. I greeted her and walked her over to her run. After putting her dinner bowl down, I closed the gate to her run and set out to bring in the last of the Mohicans.

As I neared the pasture gate, I heard a lively exchange of horse whinnies and neighs. Some of them were clearly coming from the pasture that Cherokee and Dahli Lama had come in from, while others were coming from the barn behind me. I was sure that one of the voices was Saint's. I listened with keen interest and delight to the volley of equine voices. My beloved herd was having a conversation.

Hey, where are you guys? Saint asked.

We're here, we're here in the barn. There's food. Get down here! Cherokee, or Dahli Lama, or both answered.

Less than a minute later, I spotted him emerging from the darkness. When he reached me, he didn't look the least bit surprised to see me. I knew he'd be expecting a cookie, but I also knew I had given the last of them in my pocket to Cherokee. Still, something told me to poke around in my pockets again, and when I did, I felt a single cookie in my right pocket—and not a crumb-sized one but a sizeable chunk. I wondered how that could be. The parable of loaves and fishes crossed my mind.

I was certain that Cherokee had heard my whole communication clearly, even though his herdmates didn't arrive at the same time as him. Had he chosen not to nudge the others to follow him? Had the others simply opted to take their sweet time? Or had something entirely different taken place in the pasture, to which I hadn't been privy? I couldn't say, but I knew that the entire episode had been a deeply satisfying telepathic communication.

✻

Another time, when I was in the barn giving Dahli Lama and Cherokee post-dinner treats as Saint headed out toward the east pasture, I decided to practice some telepathic communication with Cherokee. I closed the gate between him and Dahli Lama so my attention could be free of worry about being mugged for treats by her.

Then I stood about two or three feet in front of Cherokee, face-to-face with him. After briefly considering what I wanted to ask him to do, I settled on a simple action: moving his right front foot in any fashion. Before I could even convey my first message, he stretched his neck out and began conducting an active, albeit gentle, investigation of my treat-smelly clothing, focusing on my pockets. I began silently asking him to move his right foot while also sweeping my gaze from his right eye down along the right side of his neck and withers, all the way to his right front foot.

The first three times, he lifted his left leg first, followed by the right. I offered him no verbal, physical, mental, or culinary rewards on any of those occasions. At one point, he turned his head away from me, slightly toward his left. He seemed to be staring out in that direction as if he were not paying any attention to me. After several seconds, he turned back toward me and resumed sniffing my jacket pockets. I stayed still, content to accept what was taking place, and before I had a chance to silently speak to him again, he shifted his body posture, looked up, and fixed his eyes on mine.

Looking into those large brown eyes filled with such honesty, I felt how fully he was present to me, and I realized that he was waiting for me to become fully present to him so whatever I was asking of him could be clearly transmitted. It wasn't that *he* had decided to tune in more deeply to *me*. It was the other way around, and he he'd picked up on that shift, sensing that I was now energetically grounded enough to connect with him more deeply and more honestly. As we looked into each other's eyes, the world felt supremely quiet, and I was struck by how such a strong energy field could also feel very gentle and calming.

"Move your right foot," I said softly while sweeping my eye down to his foot once or twice. Within seconds, he calmly lifted his right foot and only his right foot, and I knew with certainty that we had connected at a soul level.

On another occasion, also with Cherokee, I had a profound experience of being the receiver rather than the sender of a telepathic message. After finishing up a riding and groundwork session in the round pen, I decided to listen to my inner voice, which was telling me to stay out there with Cherokee for a while longer. Standing some eight to ten feet away from Cherokee, I closed my eyes and turned my face up into the lovely autumn sunshine. I formed an intention simply to practice being with Cherokee, free of agenda or expectation. I wasn't setting up a session of telepathic communication with him, but even so, I had to practice surrendering the desire that occasionally crept in for him to come over to me.

After a time, I opened my eyes and saw that Cherokee hadn't moved or shifted his orientation at all in relation to my body. His gaze was in another direction altogether. Wanting to really dive more deeply into a practice of silent and open awareness, I thought it would be useful to sit down. So I retrieved the white mounting steps that were just outside the corral, came back inside, and placed the steps near the center of the corral. That put me a few feet closer to Cherokee.

After sitting there for a minute or so, eyes closed, I realized that my physical orientation in relation to Cherokee's body was not heart chakra to heart chakra, so I repositioned the steps, sat back down, and closed my eyes again. My mind fell quiet, blessedly empty of any desire for Cherokee to respond to my presence. After a while, I felt a strong impulse to open my eyes and look over at him.

He was staring at me quite intently and with intention, and I knew that he was beckoning me. I stood up, and as I approached him, I knew with certainty that he wanted to go back to the barn and drink water. Unlike the time we'd stood together under the tree during the retreat, the message this time hadn't come in the form of words from him to me. Instead, it had come in the form of a clear "knowingness." And not only was the message unbidden by me, but it was also simultaneous with words that spontaneously fell from my mouth. "Oh, you're ready to go back and drink some water? Okay, let's go."

Wanting to show him that I had received and understood his message, I immediately turned around and headed over to the round pen gate. Cherokee followed me, and with his lead in my hand, I led him back to the barn without making any conversation. As soon as we walked through the barn gate, I released him, and he walked directly into his own run to drink at length from the trough there.

As I watched him quenching his thirst, I reflected on some of the principles I was learning about interspecies communication. I didn't have to understand everything about how a telepathic message had come through, but I did need to acknowledge that it had come. There would be time enough to discover the ways in which I sent and received messages most efficiently and clearly. I left Cherokee in his run and walked back to the house, grateful that I'd been able to receive a message telepathically and that Cherokee had experienced having his voice heard and his request honored.

*

I continued to practice my animal communication skills, but I knew I needed much more training. So I signed up for a six-week webinar series offered by Anna Twinney, a highly regarded animal communicator and equine clinician. I arrived home from work just before the first session was about to begin and quickly powered up my computer. I watched the first thirty minutes of the webinar, avidly absorbing the content, but I was also aware that, in all likelihood, the horses were down from the pasture, awaiting their dinner. I needed to take the show on the road.

I cranked up the volume on the laptop as high as it would go, got the big bucket of prepared mash from the kitchen, and headed out to the barn, flanked, of course, by Billy and Stitch. From the front porch, I could see that all three horses were grazing outside the barn.

Even inside the main tack room, the internet connection held. But as I walked into the small confines of what I'd dubbed the ice cooler room because it held a very large ice cooler, the screen froze and the sound dropped out. I pulled out the earbuds and began the feeding routine, knowing that by the time I finished up, much of the webinar would be over. But caring for my animal relatives took priority over the webinar. It was sacrosanct.

After feeding the horses, I returned to the house and carried the laptop into the kitchen so I could catch what remained of the webinar while I fed the dogs. After about fifteen or twenty minutes, I needed to go back down to the barn to open Saint's gate. I took the laptop with me, and when I reached the fence directly in front of the stalls, I placed it on the ground near the spot where I stood to say nightly prayers.

After opening Saint's gate, I treated all three horses to the few carrot chunks I had in my pockets, whereafter Cherokee and Dahli Lama walked into Saint's run to see what leftovers might be there. Saint opted to walk around the back of the barn, making his way to the east pasture for the night. As I watched him emerge from behind the barn and head toward the lane that led to that field, the thought occurred to me that this was a golden opportunity to share some alone time with him.

"Wait for me, Saint. I'll be right there," I said aloud as I walked back to the house. "I'll give you some carrots. Wait for me!" I repeated those mantric pleas even as I crossed the living room and went into the kitchen, grabbing two apples instead of the promised carrots. Back outside, I broke into a trot and rolled myself under one of the fences.

As I neared the east pasture lane, I saw him waiting, standing about midway down the lane at a full stop. He had never before just stopped in the middle of the lane like that. But there he was, clearly waiting for me with his body angled slightly away from my approaching direction but his head turned directly toward me. I came up to him, greeted him, thanked him for waiting, and took out the first of the two apples I'd brought, telling him that he could have both apples since his herdmates weren't with us but that two small pieces would be saved in case they arrived while I was still out there. I set about biting off chunks and offering them to Saint, and once they were done, I started my usual crooning of affectionate words.

The phrase *resist the urge to word* came to mind, reminding me to stop talking words of love to him and simply be still. At that point, Saint's eye was deeply at rest in mine, and mine in his. It was the first time I'd seen that depth of connection exuding from him. And perhaps that was the first time he'd seen that depth in *my* eyes.

On my way back to the house, I stopped to retrieve the laptop from the ground. It wasn't there. Puzzled, I returned to the house and looked all around for the device. Not finding it, I walked back down to the barnyard area where I was so sure I'd left it, but just as before, it was nowhere to be found. I felt defeated and annoyed as I returned to the house.

That evening, the thought came to mind that I should try some clairsentience practice in connection with the laptop. Standing in the upstairs bathroom, I closed my eyes and waited to see what, if anything, might arise in my mind. For several minutes, I practiced letting thoughts come and go, allowing the listening to go wide, again and again. Eventually, a very clear image of Dahli Lama appeared. She was standing in the barn, tightly squeezed inside the ice cooler room.

Then the image began to move. It was like watching a black-and-white movie clip running across the screen of my mind. I saw Dahli Lama lowering her gorgeous dark grey head down to the surface of the closed ice cooler. And there was the laptop, right on top of it! And then, clear as day, I watched her muzzle nose the laptop to the left, toward the wall that separated that room and Saint's run. I watched as she nudged and nudged until the device fell into the narrow gap between the cooler and the wall.

I ran the whole way back to the barn, dashed through the main tack room and into the ice cooler room. Peering three feet down into the darkness of the gap, I saw the laptop wedged between the cooler and the wall, just as I'd seen it in my mind. Without question, Dahli Lama had sent me a message to let me know where the laptop was.

Of course, my rational mind couldn't figure or sort out how my laptop ended up in the ice cooler room when I had such a distinct memory of placing it down on the ground hours earlier. Clearly, my recollection of the chronology of events was lacking. During one of my trips to the barn, I must have placed the laptop on the ice cooler and left it there.

Still, the details of how it had gotten there didn't matter much to me, nor did the fact that the computer was still working. What mattered was that the moving picture show in my head had not been random, arbitrary, or without meaning: It had been a communication from Dahli Lama. She had picked up on my distress about the whereabouts of the laptop and sent those images to help me. It was such a gratifying experience to have been able to receive her telepathic messages.

13

Others Communicate with My Herd

Anna Twinney played an important role in my learning about interspecies animal communication, not only through my participation in her six-week webinar series, but through witnessing her in-person communications with other people's animals as well as my own. She paid a visit to my farm and communicated with my shepherd, Stitch, as well as all three horses. The time she spent with Saint was especially poignant and valuable for our relationship.

When Saint arrived, he was a somewhat aloof fellow, reticent to receive my affections. Whenever I tried to plant a kiss on his beautiful orangey-beige nose or put my arms around his neck, he would back away or turn his head. That saddened me because I was filled with a keen desire to give him the best possible life I could. I wanted him to know he was loved and was in his forever home. How could hugs and kisses not be part of the deal? It was unthinkable. He didn't even ask me for treats.

I started practicing a modified version of tough love. Essentially, that entailed "forcing" him (untethered, of course) to accept my overtures of affection in extremely short time increments—an embrace-free kiss on his nose to start with, then advancing to a neck embrace for two or three seconds. Initially, he rebuffed those overtures. But gradually, he outgrew his resistance and came around to accepting hugs, kisses, scratches, and other physical expressions of love from me. Anna Twinney's visit to the farm helped me understand more about what had been going on with Saint.

At Anna's request, I had disclosed very little about the horses. She explained that too much information would hamper her ability to assure herself that she was, in fact, connecting with the right horse. So when I filled out the pre-visit form, I only wrote a sentence or two about ages and genders and what I hoped to find out. I wanted to know if they were happy in their lives with me and whether they needed to tell me anything. That was all.

Anna began with Cherokee, followed by Saint, and then Dahli Lama. As she received what the horses were sharing, she conveyed it to me at a steady, rapid-fire pace. I jotted down what she was saying as quickly as I could. Her exchanges with all three horses not only amazed me but also helped me learn more about each horse's personality and preferences.

Her exchanges with Saint were especially emotional for me and, it seemed, for Saint as well. He told her certain things that I had previously sensed about him, not through telepathy but from observing his body language and his behavior toward me at specific times. For instance, he confided to her his difficulty with receiving affection. "He wants you to know that it's hard for him to be held around the neck, especially the right side, but he is really trying," she reported. He also told her he had never had a "special" person.

As Anna told me this last bit, she was tearing up, though right after she said it, she paused, looked up at me, and said, "These are not my tears." With that, she dropped her head back down, closed her eyes, and resumed her communication with Saint. I took her comment to mean that the welling up of emotion had come from Saint himself. That was a heartbreaking revelation, but I had to keep my focus on scribbling down the rest of their exchange.

When their session came to a close, Anna lifted her head and sat back in her chair. I waited silently. She turned to me and said she had a few additional comments to make on Saint's behalf. "Saint will be fine with children," she began. "Children can be over him, under him, and generally all around him. That all will be fine."

I took in the information with a mixture of awe at the whole process of interspecies communication and concern about my complete lack of connection to any young children. "Uh, huh. Okay," I replied.

"But you are going to have to protect him and keep him safe." she added. "This means setting boundaries for him. He's a very dear fellow. He really is. And he will want to please you. He won't find it easy to say no to requests made of him. You will need to take good care of him in that regard. Do you understand?"

"Yes. Yes, I do. Yes, I understand. Thank you." I replied.

From that day on, I started quietly telling him, "I'm your special person. I'm the one. I'm your special person." It became part of my repertoire, another ingredient added to the daily cocktail of love, affection, and treats. I was so happy when he finally felt at home and secure enough to start mugging me for those handfuls!

But Anna wasn't the only person to communicate with my horses besides me. Some, like my trainer and friend Bill, communicated with them on a regular basis and others, like my friend and former bandmate Dave, less frequently. Dave's experiences with the herd allowed me to see that interspecies communication took many forms and often involved people who didn't necessarily name it as such.

About a year after the move to the farm, Dave drove to Colorado from New Jersey to spend several days with the herd and me. He enjoyed a generous amount of time alone with the horses, and I received a letter from him about it afterward. The sense of connection and bonding he experienced with the horses on one day in particular was much more profound than he had expected, and he wanted to thank me for letting him be in charge of the property and all the animals while I was at work down in Denver.

That day, a light snow was falling. Dave went out to the barn, intending to muck the runs, wheel the poop out a designated area of the west pasture, and then stay out there to take some pictures. The horses were in their runs, standing far enough back so that the snow wasn't falling on them. Their runs were nearly clean, so he took the half-filled wheelbarrow out to the west pasture and dumped its load. Then he headed farther out into the pasture, toward the top of the ridge, to get some photos from that vantage point.

As he began to climb up the ridge, he looked back and saw all three horses at the open gate to the pasture, watching him. When he reached the top of the ridge, he looked back again, but the horses were out of sight from that angle. He spent a few minutes taking some pictures, and then sensed that he wasn't alone. He turned and saw Cherokee, Saint, and Dahli Lama making their way to him. They formed a circle around him and stood there, watching and listening to him as he began to talk, thanking them for letting him be a part of their herd for the past several days. When Dahli nudged him a few times, he took it as her way of letting him know she liked his company.

He told them he was leaving the next day and charged them with taking care of me. Cherokee seemed to react to that because he came right up to Dave's face and looked him in the eye intently. Dave was certain that Cherokee had understood his request. One by one, the horses began to drift off, biting at the hay that was poking through the snow. He left them to their grazing and came back down to the barn with the wheelbarrow by stepping through the path created by the herd's hooves.

I got a little choked up as I read Dave's closing comments. "I thank you for opening my eyes to this otherwise unknown universe. Growing up watching cowboy movies put me in the mindset that horses were just big dogs. I've found (through you) that they are much, much more."

My herd was impacting interspecies relationships one human at a time, and my friend, Renee, was another human who was deeply impacted by their presence. She came to some important realizations while in their company. And like Dave, she sent me a thank-you letter a few days later. It was a detailed,

emotionally rich description of the time she spent with Cherokee, Saint, and, most especially, Dahli Lama.

Renee was living in a typical suburban neighborhood in
Boulder, and I had extended her an open invitation to drive
over and spend some solitary time on my property, whether or
not I was home. One day she took me up on it and had a very
inspirational time with the horses—Dahli Lama in particular.

That day, as she walked along a trail that ran alongside one
of the fields, she saw that the horses had noticed her but didn't
seem to be paying her any mind. She stopped at a spot that felt
right for doing her ceremonial work "to call in my right life,"
as she put it. With the horses in view across the field, she sat
down and placed her sacred items on the land. As she began to
deepen into the calling in her heart, she heard the horses gal-
loping toward her. When she looked up, there were three sets
of curious noses and witnessing eyes pointed right at her. She
burst out laughing and thought, *Oh, now that I'm about to tell the
truth, you're interested in me, eh?*

Her ceremony was a calling for bringing her dreams into
manifestation, and a part of that was opening her home as a
retreat center for people to do spiritual work with her or to stay
there while in their own program of inner work. She especially
had Melisa Pearce's Touched by a Horse certification program
in mind and heart. She could really taste the honor of hosting
those who were doing that work and felt it would be a rich
blessing for them and for her.

The horses "saw that the ceremony was good," Renee said,
and walked off. But Dahli Lama then turned around and came
back, and Renee sensed that the mare had something to contrib-

ute to the ceremony. She gave her full attention to Dahli Lama, who insisted on scratches in front of and directly behind her ears. Renee complied with that request for what seemed like a full hour, and whenever she stopped scratching, Dahli Lama immediately nudged her back into action, and also lowered her head frequently to make it easier on Renee's arms.

Renee found Dahli Lama to be a sweet equine partner who not only taught her how to do an ear scratch *correctly* (that was the word she heard Dahli Lama say to her), but also performed some energy work on Renee's heart chakra. Renee described how she could feel her body and mind recognizing the need to make vital changes in her life, acknowledging the need to spend more time with horses, nature, and silence. As she let her heart open to receive Dahli Lama's energetic offerings, she felt a strong need to have her home become a sacred retreat center and saw that this would have the added benefit of allowing her and her son to live by themselves, without housemates.

And there were other awarenesses that Renee experienced in Dahli Lama's company. She had songs to compose, spiritual concerts to give, inspirational talks to offer, and books to write. *I trust God. Bring it on*, she thought.

When she heard "sacred neighs" from the other two horses across the field soon after this, she felt validated in her new awarenesses. She also knew that it was the right time to close her ceremony. During her drive back home to Boulder, Renee experienced the emotional aftermath of her time in the company of the herd. "I was butter by the time our soul striving, our scratching ceremony, was complete," she said. "That evening as I drove home, I was thinking of Dahli Lama's amazing beingness while listening to an exquisite song. I unexpectantly burst into sobs and had to pull over because I couldn't see the road. To this moment, I still don't know if I was crying or laughing or both. I was just in it until it was done with me."

Two days after her sacred time at my place, Renee asked Spirit to give her a clear sign that she was on the right track and could have what she had set her intention on. Later that same day, she received an inquiry from a Touched by a Horse staff member asking, for the first time, if she had any room availability for three students who were coming into town to attend a weekend training. Since she had asked Spirit that very morning to give her a clear sign that she was on the right track and could have what she had set her intention on, it was clear to Renee that Spirit had answered her in the clearest of terms.

But it took a little help from Dahli Lama to get the ball rolling.

14

Healings for the Horses and Me

As I worked through the TBAH certification program and settled into my relationships with my horses, my understanding of the word *healing* expanded considerably, particularly in the context of interactions between horses and humans. Whether a horse was the recipient of a healing by a human, or vice versa, it was nothing short of astonishing to witness the depth of understanding and sensitivity that horses brought to these encounters.

In August of 2011, I attended one of several clinics needed to achieve my certification. By then, I was about halfway through the program and had spent many hours in the company of Melisa's horses, observing how they accurately gauged the emotional temperature of the student being coached. (A horseman I know once put it this way: Horses are excellent bullshitometers!) It was remarkable to see how quickly the partnering horse inside the round pen came over to the rails closest to the area where coach and client were sitting just outside the enclosure, engaging in the early part of that coaching session.

I watched in amazement as the horse listened intently through the rails and then, once the student was inside with him or her, went to work on the next part of the process, allowing the exploration of issues and unfinished business to deepen. At the same time, the student, as well as the rest of us in attendance, progressed in our training as future equine Gestalt coaches.

When we broke for lunch that day, the rest of the group filtered out of the arena and headed over to the long buffet table to fill their plates and spread out on the beautiful grounds to eat. I stayed seated in my chair. It wasn't that I'd been especially impacted by the morning session or craved some alone time. I just felt a strong desire to walk over to the horses, and I knew it was an impulse I needed to obey.

I crossed the sandy arena and started walking down the aisle. As I peered into each of the long runs, I didn't have any particular member of the herd in mind or heart. Most of the seven or eight horses were standing close to the near end of their stalls and approached the rails to greet me. I spoke softly to each one before moving on. When I got to the second to last one, Fancy's stall, I saw that she, too, was standing a few feet back from the rails. But unlike her herdmates, she didn't come over to the rails to greet me, nor did she show any curiosity about me. She kept her distance, which didn't surprise me since I knew she was a serious-minded seventeen-year-old mare not given to lavish affection or schmoozing with the students with whom she interacted.

What she *was* given to was one form of energy work in particular. Fancy was one of Melisa's chief chakra balancers. And while she was wonderfully skilled in that healing modality, she wasn't always perfectly adroit in her physical movements while cofacilitating coaching sessions. Every so often, she would inadvertently step on the foot of the student around whom she was maneuvering her sizeable Gypsy Vanner frame. Once she was done with her work, she quietly turned away from her client, neither awaiting thanks nor offering further communion. Eschewing social niceties, Fancy directed her energies toward diligent and efficient healing work.

After standing in the aisle outside her stall for a minute or so, I felt a strong impulse to venture in. This was a highly unusual thing to do at a clinic, since students only went into the horses' runs to bring them in and out for coaching sessions, safety demonstrations, showers, or grooming. At the end of each clinic day, some of us volunteered to stay behind to distribute hay and grains to the herd. But even that didn't involve entering their stalls since they all had large metal stall feeders that swung open to the aisle for filling.

Fancy wasn't an excitable mare. Still, I had no idea how she would react to my entering her personal space. We had been taught by Melisa that a horse's personal space "bubble" extended out at least fifteen feet. That meant that once I entered Fancy's stall, I would already be standing well within her personal space. Melisa had also impressed upon us the importance of letting horses know you were about to enter that space, and if the horse was not already familiar with you, it was important to gain their acknowledgment and consent before doing so. That had immediately resonated with me, and I adopted it as a rule of etiquette.

I opened the gate and went inside. Walking slowly but not

furtively, I went over to Fancy and extended my left hand, palm down, for her to sniff. With my right hand, I stroked her left side. Although she didn't seem especially interested in my presence or touch, I was pleased with our initial interaction. Then I walked deeper into her stall and then out to her run. The hot, dry Colorado sun felt delicious.

Approaching the rails that separated Fancy's run from Tori's, I greeted the latter mare. She was only too happy to return the greeting, which was no surprise since Tori was Melisa's go-to horse when students or private clients needed powerful heart-healing energy. Just as Fancy excelled at balancing chakras, Tori helped people release pain connected to bereavement, loss, abandonment, or brokenheartedness. Tori had suffered the loss of multiple babies, either through miscarriage or having them taken from her in their infancy. So she was all too familiar with losses of the hardest kind.

During one of the clinics I attended, Tori had been held back from participating in any of the coaching pieces. Melisa explained that she had been keeping a close watch on Tori for the past few days and had been communicating with the horse on deep levels. She knew that her generous mare was experiencing her own crisis of the heart and felt it would be unfair to ask her to deal with anyone else's mental or emotional needs at that time. Although Tori appeared physically sound with no apparent signs of colic or other distress, she wasn't eating. Melisa was very concerned about that and gratefully allowed Tori to be treated to multiple Reiki sessions by two students, Dana and Dawn, who were master level practitioners. Happily, by the final day of the clinic, Tori had perked up significantly, as evidenced by her willingness to start eating and engaging with the humans around her.

I began stroking Tori's nose through the rails, and I could tell from the way she was taking in my presence that she wasn't merely checking me out. She was transmitting waves of love to me and into me, giving me a generous helping of her huge heartfulness. A big wave of emotion came over me then, and I began sobbing. With my head tilted up to the sky, I found myself crying out, "I want to do right by my horses. I want to do right by my horses. I want to do right by my horses." Whether it was a plea, a prayer, or an affirmation, I repeated those words again and again.

At some point, I became aware of a presence just off my right shoulder. It was Fancy. She had come over to offer *her* brand of energy work. I continued stroking Tori with my left hand and started stroking Fancy with my right one, turning myself slightly in her direction. Eventually, I turned myself fully around to face her and lowered my arms so my energy and awareness could be directed solely to bearing witness and receiving. And yet, all the while, my pleas kept sounding and my tears kept falling. Those things were beyond my control.

In her characteristically unsubtle fashion, Fancy proceeded to thrust herself into me, using various areas of her body. She primarily gave me a lot of root (first) chakra and solar plexus (third) chakra, the former being connected to security and well-being and the latter with will and determination. She offered very little heart (fourth) chakra, which made perfect sense to me, for in truth, I wasn't lacking in heart connections with my three horses. That wonderful Gypsy Vanner was aware that my heart chakra wasn't where I needed her vibrational help.

At one point, her root chakra offering was pressing into me so forcefully that had someone been watching without an understanding of what was going on, they might have feared for my physical welfare. Fancy was pressing her buttocks— the body area associated with the general location of *her* root chakra—very firmly up against my front torso, effectively sandwiching me between her rear end and the rails. Unafraid, I received her offering with unfettered gratitude. I was still crying up to the heavens, though my pleas had become silent.

Then Fancy started doing something I had never see her do before. Had that same imaginary observer not been overly concerned earlier, they would likely have become understandably alarmed then. Fancy began grinding her buttocks back and forth against my chest. The pressure was exquisite. After several grindings, she stopped and maneuvered her hefty draft body around so her left side directly faced me and her head faced the arena. After giving one parting shot of will and determination to my front torso, she turned away and paid me no further heed. We were done. She had brought the session to a close in her typically unceremonious fashion.

After collecting myself for a few moments, I thanked both horses for their care and walked back through the arena and out to the food service area. I had no desire to speak to anyone or even be in their close company, so I filled a plate and took myself off to a quiet spot by the pond for the duration of our break.

In her inimitable way, Fancy had not only cleared my chakras, she'd also given me an important message: *Just keep going, Nancy. Your heart is in the right place. Just keep going.*

Fancy wasn't the only horse to offer me a chakra clearing that deeply affected me. Dahli Lama has had her way with my chakras too. Besides the alignments she offered me that first day I was alone with her at the breeding ranch in Ault, there were other occasions when she did that kind of energy work on me. One afternoon, I brought her out to the round pen, undecided if we were going to do some groundwork or just hang out for a while. I figured I'd see what arose after grounding myself in the center of the ring. When I opened my eyes, Dahli Lama was standing right in front of me, facing me. I stroked her velvety nose and admired, as always, that perfectly shaped diamond on her forehead.

Then I went out to the rails and started walking in a counterclockwise direction, and Dahli Lama followed me, staying a respectful foot or so off of my left shoulder as we went along. We made several rotations in alternating directions and also cut through the middle a few times. When we came to a stop in the center, I rubbed her neck and told her what a good girl she was.

Then things took an unusual and unforgettable turn. Dahli Lama started sniffing and nuzzling me all over. Her energy was very focused and intentional, as though she were searching for a lost object or wondering what my scent reminded her of. Her contact with my skin was very firm. She even took occasional nips on various parts of my body. I wasn't frightened by this, especially since I wasn't feeling teeth, just lips and gums. After each of these nips, she tossed her head up and over to her left side and opened her mouth. Then she went back to noodling me with her muzzle. It was quite a medley of behaviors.

As we carried on, I reprimanded her a few times when I

could actually feel her teeth pressing ever so slightly against—though not into—my skin. On those occasions, I pulled my head back, looked her straight in the eye, and poked her two or three times under one of her eyes. Then she went back to pressing her nose and mouth onto my chest and arms and even my hands. It was as if she and I were having a conversation about boundaries.

Is this okay?

Yes, that's fine.

How about this?

No, that's going too far.

Can I get away with this?

No, not that.

Oh, I like doing this!

Okay, I like it too.

After a while, Dahli Lama moved her strenuous body scanning, sniffing, and licking up to my hair and scalp. That startled me. Although I'd seen one or two of Melisa's horses work on the crown of a student's head, what Dahli Lama was doing seemed more vigorous than that. She even began to nip the top of my head lightly, but in a way that was wholly nonthreatening. I wasn't hurt in any way by these nips, nor was there was any ear-pinning or other worrisome behaviors. I reminded myself to relax, breathe, feel my feet on the ground, and stay present to what was happening instead of getting involved with a host of circling thoughts about it. Although I had my own eyes closed for much of that part of the session, I could see how soft hers were whenever I looked up into them.

After staying up at my crown for some time, she wrapped

her head around me and pulled me in close, right up against her neck. Then she ran her jawline and the underside of her head up my spine and back down. She did that once more and then stopped. I felt wonderful bodily releases after both of those outrageous adjustments.

When I released her from the round pen and watched her rejoin her herdmates, I felt quietly elated and profoundly grateful. I realized that by trusting in Dahli Lama's good intentions with those mouth movements, sniffs, nips, and head tosses, I had opened the way for our pas de deux to become a thorough session of energy work. And something else dawned on me: That nipping at the top of my head had been a clearing of my crown chakra, Dahli Lama-style!

I felt an incredible lightness of spirit afterward, and I knew it was attributable to Dahli Lama's healing work with me. As I walked the path back to the house, I had no desire to analyze what I was feeling. I wanted to let it be, not let my mind trample all over the sense of ease. I acknowledged how blessed I felt to have received this equine laying on of hands and left it at that.

I was on the receiving end of the healing that day, but there have been times when I was able to be the one providing the healing. For two brief periods across a couple of years, Cherokee developed an unsettling change in behavior: He flat out refused to let me touch his left ear, the left side of his face, or the left side of his neck. Hugs were out of the question. If I attempted to touch any of those regions, he spooked, abruptly moving his head and neck out of reach. As far as I could tell, nothing untoward had happened to him in the days leading up to that behavior.

As with all equine matters that perplexed or concerned me, I talked it over with Bill during each of these periods. His best guess was that memories of past abuse were resurfacing and asserting control over Cherokee, though he didn't discount the possibility that Cherokee had somehow strained the left side of his upper body on those occasions. It saddened me terribly to see my sweet fellow weighed down by this impediment of uncertain genesis. My gut told me it was more emotional than physical, but if that speculation was accurate, why and how had those memories erupted seemingly overnight like that each time?

It was a discouraging mystery. Whenever any odd behaviors or physical symptoms arise in one of my animal relatives, I can become overwhelmed by a sense of urgency about figuring out the what, why, and how of a situation. But I also know that solving an enigma concerning the horses isn't necessarily a precursor for my taking action on their behalf. Sometimes I just have to trust my instincts.

During one of those distressing periods, I draped the lead over the left side of Cherokee's neck, down at the base, carefully nudged it up a bit, and walked him out to the round pen to do some groundwork. But once we were out there, I felt an impulse to spend the time quietly hanging out with him. I went with my gut and skipped our formal training.

Standing very close to him on his left side, I reached up to touch him with my right hand, taking care to confine myself to regions farther down on his left side. He was fine with me stroking his left shoulder and withers. At some point, I intentionally let my hand venture into the forbidden zone and began stroking him there. "Can you let go of the past?" I asked him softly after a few minutes. I repeated the question twice more.

All the while, Cherokee's head continued to face forward. He didn't spook. His left eye, the only one I could see, didn't look especially soft, but it didn't look panicked either. It looked alert. I could see that he was taking in the energetic field around him, sensing my good intentions. His demeanor quietly conveyed that he felt safe and there was no need to flee.

I let my hand come to rest on his neck and had an inner understanding that I needed to surrender even the subtlest expectation about what should come next. I needed to allow for all the inner portals and pathways in both of us to be as open and unimpeded as possible. The air felt thick with possibility. I took a moment to acknowledge this sense of potentiality, then I reconnected to the feel of my hand on Cherokee's neck. I knew, without claiming it in some prideful way, that I was simply an instrument of healing with nothing to do but have faith in what was taking place, free of inner commentary.

After some time, Cherokee dropped his head and neck way down low and stayed there for some time. In and of itself, that was deeply gratifying because that yielding position wasn't one that Cherokee typically assumed. It was an unmistakable sign of security and trust. And beyond that, I knew a healing had taken place.

When Bill stopped by to check on things a few days later, Cherokee seemed more relaxed about his left side but not fully so. I stepped away and observed from a distance to afford the two of them their own space. Bill placed his hands on two "safe" areas of Cherokee's body and stood there silently for several minutes. When he took his hands away, he said he had a sense of which of the Bach Flower Remedies might come to Cherokee's aid. When he returned the next day with the mixture he'd concocted, I watched closely as he administered the first dose into Cherokee's mouth. For the next seven or eight days, I followed that same protocol. Then I flew to New York for a brief preplanned family visit.

When I returned, I was greeted by a horse who received my left-side embraces without issue. It was the perfect welcome home. Clearly, Cherokee had been relieved of whatever the issue was, at least for then.

I hoped it was for good, but that wasn't the case. A year and a half later, the same sensitivity reappeared with an added element: Cherokee balked at my even approaching his left side. I was puzzled not only by the reemergence of this behavior, but also by the seeming uptick in his anxiety. Rather than work in small increments to help him regain his composure when touched in those areas, I wondered if there was a way to help him release whatever emotional blockages were afflicting him once and for all.

I had recently completed Reiki training for levels one and two under the guidance of a wonderful instructor, Gianna Settin, and it occurred to me that I should employ Reiki. Standing a foot or so away from Cherokee, I gently dropped the halter and lead down and took a minute to ground myself. Then I silently invoked Reiki energy, using the words Gianna had taught me: Without ego, personality, or expectation, I invoked Reiki for Cherokee's highest welfare. I checked in with myself, making sure my hands, mind, and heart were free from any goals in connection with Cherokee's left side. Then I held my hands up in Reiki position a foot or so from the left side of Cherokee's face.

At first, he stared straight ahead. But in less than a minute, he made certain motions with his mouth known as "licking and chewing." There are different schools of thought about what that behavior indicates. Some folks view it as a sign of relaxation. Others believe the horse is mulling things over, not only to comprehend what is being asked of him or her, but also to assess whether or not the requested action is one to which he or she is willing to acquiesce. I'd observed both of those at different times when my horses expressed licking and chewing behavior.

I spent a good amount of time with Cherokee, my sole intention being to practice Reiki as sincerely and purely as possible. Well into the session, he turned and lowered his head to get at the kibble treats in my waist pouch. That had the effect of causing his left ear to graze my hands. After it happened several times without flinching on his part, I decided to gently cup my hand around the back of his ear while he munched the treats. He stayed calm throughout, with no signs of concern. We stayed like that until it felt like the right time to bring things to a close. I acknowledged to both of us and to Spirit that the Reiki offering was complete and released all the horses from their runs.

Interestingly, Cherokee chose to stay by himself in the field surrounding the barn while Saint and Dahli Lama grazed in close proximity to one another elsewhere in the same field. That configuration was highly uncharacteristic of the herd. Even more surprising, for much of the evening, Cherokee remained in that same field while his herdmates left to walk over to another enclosed paddock a hundred or so yards away. Was he integrating the healing, or did he just need some solitary contemplative time? I didn't know.

My handsome fellow has had no further signs of that difficulty, and my gut tells me it is gone for good. But should it arise again, I will stand by his side and we will sort it out together, at a pace that he will dictate. And I will, of course, have treats on hand.

I've had the opportunity to do a bit of healing work with my other two horses too. A couple of months after Anna Twinney's visit to the farm, I was standing outside of Saint's run, waiting for him to finish up his dinner so I could set him free. I opened his gate and stood at the far end. But when he was done eating, he stayed put instead of heading out to pasture. I approached him on his left side and began speaking to him in a soft voice. "Good boy, Saint. Good boy. You're going to be with me forever. I'm your special person. I'm the one. Good boy. Good boy."

Then I started talking to him about something new that was connected to what he had conveyed to Anna. "If you want to be around children, Saint, we can have you give them kiddie rides. If you want to have that purpose in life, I'll take good care of you. I promise I'll protect you. I won't let anyone on you that you don't want on you. And I won't let anyone hurt you. Do you think that's something you might like to do? It's okay if you don't."

His left eye, the only one I could see, was soft and liquid. After a minute or two, he turned his head slightly to the left, toward me. That eye looked softer than I had ever seen it, and his body posture and whole demeanor showed that he was relaxed and attentive. Twice, he nodded his head while I was talking to him about the kiddie rides. But even after I stopped speaking, Saint still made no move to turn around and head for the open gate.

I reached out my right arm and began massaging his neck in small effleurage circles. He seemed to like that, so I moved around to stand directly in front of his jowl area, allowing me to massage both sides of his neck and get nice and high, near the base of his ears. I was gratified by how relaxed he was. He even did something that, up to that point, I'd only experienced with Cherokee: He dropped his head onto me, and I felt the rather astonishingly heavy weight of it pressing down into my left shoulder. Luckily, every once in a while, he lifted his head for a few moments, affording me a much-needed opportunity to reposition and strengthen my footholds. I also moved to alternate sides of his neck a few times to give each of my shoulders a break. Basically, I was hanging on by the curl of my toes, scrunching them into the hardened earth as best I could.

About fifteen minutes in, the two of us volleyed what I would call a medley of releases. It started with Saint letting out a huge sigh—long, loud, and glorious. That was immediately followed by *my* body releasing a tiny puff of gas which, in turn, was followed by Saint's body releasing a luxuriously long stream of gas. Bodily functions exchanged, we resumed as before, my hands massaging with light effleurage as Saint's head pressed down on my shoulder with even heavier pressure than before. I thought he might actually be falling asleep. It was a sweet contemplation.

The spell was eventually broken by Billy's intermittent barking, but I felt no pangs of disappointment or annoyance. Saint and I had shared a satisfyingly full communion by then. That was the measure, and the measure was perfect.

15

My Horses, My Partners

When I began doing coaching work, I started browsing the aisles of thrift shops, searching out items that could potentially be used as props or aids during the sessions: a birthday cone hat, a wand, a crown, a gigantic stuffed rabbit, a bunch of plastic flowers. One item I nearly always had with me was Melisa Pearce's *Whispers from a Horse's Heart* card deck. I didn't necessarily use it in every coaching session, though. Gestalt coaching involved being in the moment, checking in with the client, and letting knowledge arise about which aides might be useful. And whether or not I used the cards in any given coaching session, I liked using them for my personal reflection practices.

Another object I kept on hand for possible use with clients was an unusual necklace I picked up at a local yard sale in Longmont. I dubbed it my "Presence Ball." It was a shiny, silver metallic ball, larger than a gumball but smaller than a golf ball. It had a shimmery reflective quality to it with flecks and flashes of gold, green, silver, and pink, and it hung on a long black cord. The pièce de résistance: When you shook the ball or gave it a quick finger flick, it emitted a marvelous gong-like tone that was richly baritone and not the least bit tinny.

As soon as I saw it, I knew it would be a great coaching tool. I could sit down with a client, give the ball a shake, and then we could practice staying in the present moment together as we listened all the way through the sound. That wouldn't take very long since it only reverberated for three or four seconds. It would serve as a quick hit of presence—a good way to begin a coaching session. I also figured I could use it in my everyday life as a piece of jewelry, stopping occasionally to give it a jingle and a listen, making it a piece of jewelry that was also a wake-up tool.

It was a good thing I trusted my instincts and bought that necklace. Not long after that, I had a visionary experience with it that helped me create an important element of my equine coaching business. It happened while I was in the downstairs bathroom at the farmhouse, sitting on the toilet. I glanced down at how my new necklace was lying in a crevice of my pajama top and saw a vision reflected in the shiny ball. It was a horse standing in a field, showing his right-face profile, exposing his "far side." There was a faceless woman standing on the near side of the horse with her head resting on the horse's back, looking out over the horse's far side. The image shifted then, and what came into focus was that same faceless woman sitting in a lotus position within the inside curve of the horse's reclining body.

I realized that I was looking at the perfect logo for my equine coaching business! It would be the image of a horse lying down in a field with her head upright and her body curved around in a half circle. There would be a woman sitting in a lotus position inside the curvature of the horse. The woman's eyes would be closed in meditation, and the horse's eyes would be open, looking out into the distance over the woman's head. I also saw mountain ranges behind the two of them.

The vision was clearly defined and lingered for so long that afterward, I had no trouble accurately reproducing it on paper. Delighted, I emailed my rudimentary sketches to my daughter, Hannah, an artist, for her consideration and refinement. I was deeply satisfied that this important piece of my equine coaching business had fallen into place. It reminded me of the proclamation I had uttered at the horse retreat: "Believe the vision."

As my graduation from the TBAH training program neared, it was time to move from education into action—from Melisa's arena and her horses to my round pen and my herd. I needed to trust my capacity to hold space for people coming for coaching sessions and trust that my herd instinctively knew what to do. The wisdom card deck, the Presence Ball, and all the other props I had collected would be secondary to the most important components of this work: the horses and me. I began offering workshops for small groups of people, as well as one-on-one private sessions.

Saint and Tamara

When my friend Tamara came for an equine coaching session, we began by sitting in chairs facing each other. I didn't have my Presence Ball with me that particular day, so I guided us through a stillness practice: feeling our bodies in the chair; experiencing the play of air on the skin; and allowing the listening to go wide and any arising thoughts to fall away. Saint, the elder statesman of the herd, was already in the round pen a few feet away, within easy earshot of our conversation.

After a few minutes, I reached for the wisdom card deck and invited Tamara to pick a card and read it, either aloud or to herself. She chose the card titled "Mystical," shared it with me in its entirety, and remarked that she really liked the part about cleansing her thoughts and converting her energy to the greater good. When she mentioned something about wanting to get rid of her limiting beliefs about herself, what arose in my mind was an image of her plucking and tossing down blossoms and petals from a bouquet of plastic flowers I had as she circled the outside of the round pen.

I retrieved the bouquet from the barn, handed it to Tamara, and directed her to start walking around the outside perimeter of the round pen while sounding aloud or silently the stem sentences *I surrender* and *I release*, completing them with whatever did not serve her highest good. I also invited her to toss away those limiting ideas as represented by the plastic petals and blossoms.

It was beautiful to witness the earnestness with which Tamara approached her task. Her pace was unhurried and deliberate. During the session, she silently walked a few feet, paused to reflect before plucking and tossing down a piece or two from the bouquet, and then resumed her walk.

Throughout the session, I kept an eye on Saint. Initially, he stayed put on the far side of the round pen from where Tamara had taken her first steps forward. But I could see that all the while, he was calmly taking note of her actions as he consumed the few stalks of hay strewn on the ground. Then, as Tamara came around to the corral panel nearest Saint during her first rotation, he looked up from his grazing and stood stock-still for the several seconds it took for Tamara to speak her truth silently and toss down a blossom. When she resumed her walk, Saint immediately came up alongside her and matched his pace to hers as they circled around together. When she stopped, he stopped; when she walked, he walked.

After a while, Tamara walked over to me and sat down. Before I could ask if she wanted to join Saint in the round pen, she said she wanted to talk about what had taken place. She was clearly excited, and I welcomed the prospect of hearing all about it. The first thing she said was that giving her the bouquet to carry had been perfect.

"The big white flowers represented the purity of my ancestors," she said, adding that she had honored them during her walk. "And these things," she continued, pointing to some of the plastic yellow buds, "these are the thorns and thorny things I surrendered and released."

She was beaming, and I was struck by the wisdom she had expressed. In her description, she used a triad of words: honor, surrender, and release. Because it seemed important to do so, I repeated them back to her, making sure that she acknowledged that it was *her* wisdom. In response, Tamara commented that it was another example of threes in her life. She noted a few examples, among them the fact that she had not only rescued three horses but had given each of them a name that began with the letter S.

Air-drawing in the space between us, I said that the words holding such meaning for her could be physically represented as a triad:

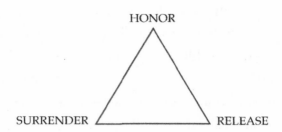

I assured her that it was fine if that imagery didn't resonate with her, but from the way she was grinning, it was clear she found value in it. Well, that and the fact that she was clapping her hands in front of her face.

I invited her to join Saint inside the round pen and take a few moments to become still. Even before she reached the center to do that, Saint was approaching her. I asked her to walk around the inside perimeter while continuing to work with those same two stem sentences. Saint followed her over to the rails and circled around with her the whole time, staying just off her inside shoulder. She continued to work silently, and when they crossed back into the center after a few rotations, Saint moved really close to her and placed his head right next to hers. They stayed like that for several minutes as I watched in silence.

I asked Tamara if there was anything that might not yet have been honored, surrendered, or released. "Yes," she replied without hesitation. "There *is* more. And I do want to work with that as well."

We paused together for a few moments while Saint stood very still a few feet away from her, directly facing her. His connection to her was unmistakable. It occurred to me that I should retrieve the bouquet lying nearby on the ground and bring it to Tamara. I placed it at her feet and then repositioned it slightly so the white flowers—her ancestors—weren't touching the dirt. She smiled in appreciation when I explained that. I invited her to either pick up the bouquet and resume tossing petals and blossoms or leave it be.

She walked over to the rails with the bouquet and began circling around, either remaining silent or speaking aloud so quietly that I couldn't hear her. Initially, Saint stayed put in the center, but as soon she came around behind him, he turned his whole body around to face her, took one small step toward her, and stopped. At that point, Tamara wasn't directly facing him. Three things happened in quick sequence then. First, Saint lifted his tail and passed gas. Then he made some mouth and tongue movements, known as "leaching" in our equine coaching circle, that indicated he was experiencing energetic releases that probably related to emotional blockages in Tamara she had been letting go of during her walk. Saint then lowered his head all the way to the ground.

I was so struck by the releases that I felt compelled to break into the silent flow of events. I wanted to check in with Tamara about whether anything particularly powerful had been going on for her in the last few minutes. So I quietly asked her how she was doing, and when she looked over at me, there were tears on her face and in her eyes. I commented that she must have been doing some heavy releasing during her walk, described Saint's actions, and pointed out that he seemed to have been mirroring her process.

Tamara rejoined Saint in the center of the ring, and in the tradition I created early in my equine coaching work, I asked Tamara to please share with Saint some of the qualities she recognized in him. This was one of my favorite parts of having clients spend time with my horses. She did that, and as she was leaving the round pen, she paused at the gate and said, "Wow, I'm so exhausted."

She came back to her chair, drank some water, and commented on the remarkable artwork on the card she had picked. She also noted how moved she had been by the whole session. The card went home with her as a remembrance of the awarenesses and releases she had experienced during the session.

That she had felt a bit spent was understandable. By embracing the session so fully, she had done some deep inner work. Time and again, I had seen how emotional releases affected the whole of a person, including the physical body.

Looking over at Tamara, I could tell from her grin, her bright eyes, and her relaxed posture that it was the really good kind of exhaustion.

Cherokee and Linda

There was something particularly fulfilling about working with fellow TBAH students while I was going through my certification process. One of the ways we supported each other was by getting together at one of our homes (or barns where our horses were boarded) to engage in coaching pieces with each other. Another way was by allowing fellow students to make use of our horses and our properties to conduct coaching sessions with their own clients. That happened a couple of times at my Longmont property, and on one of those occasions, I had the privilege of being a participant. It was an extremely meaningful and educational experience for me.

Fellow student, Ashara, had been over to my place once before and had partnered with a very young Dahli Lama to do some work with one of her clients. This time, she was going to work with a different client, and I was going to participate as both her horse handler and a member of the sacred circle. Along with her husband, Glenn, and her client, Linda—another student in the TBAH program—we were a group of four adults.

For this session, it was Cherokee who was brought out to the round pen. In the opening circle, Linda spoke of her extreme dissatisfaction with both her employment and her romantic circumstances. Her session was going to revolve around what she identified as the twin themes of shedding what no longer served her truest self and gaining the freedom to step out as a new person.

At Ashara's request, an oddball assortment of objects found on the grounds and in the barn were commissioned for use in the piece of work. The three of us walked a short distance away while Ashara considered what might come next. We waited patiently, and then, in the beautiful way that Gestalt coaching works when everyone stays open to the process, the next step presented itself to Ashara. She had Glenn and me retrieve a nearby wheelbarrow and two large tarps. The experiment was afoot.

Glenn and I became a large steel wall with one of the tarps. Ashara directed Linda to stand before the wall and connect to her solar plexus, the area of the body where the third chakra, which influences one's will and determination, is located. A few minutes into the somatic exercise, Ashara instructed Linda to stay connected to her inner strength and intentionality and melt her way through the wall.

Linda broke through to the other side of our wall and made a few comments, which gave rise to Ashara's idea for a second experiment. Using a second tarp, Glenn and I now morphed into a tall *brick* wall. Ashara invited Linda to disassemble this "wall of limitations" while sounding aloud the name of each brick or what it represented. Rather than being actual red bricks, made from sand and broken glass, these were comprised of Linda's negative thoughts, feelings, recollections, and somatic awarenesses.

As Linda pulled each brick out of our wall, she spoke. "All the bad decisions I've made." Pull. "I'm not good enough as I am." Pull. "Frustration." Pull. This went on for some time, brick by brick, until Linda stepped back and announced that the whole wall had crumbled to the ground. Glenn and I enacted this by stooping down and allowing the tarp to drop to our feet. Watching Linda carry out this task so bravely and earnestly reminded me of the trials that Pamina and Tamino underwent in *The Magic Flute*. I loved being one of the set pieces in this unfolding experiment.

After Linda told us she felt complete, Ashara pointed to the nearby wheelbarrow. "Load up all the bricks into that pickup truck and dispose of them for all time," she instructed.

Once that was done, Linda was invited to go into the round pen and was charged with the task of greeting Cherokee as a new person who was free of those limiting and false beliefs.

Linda entered the round pen and stopped some distance from Cherokee. For his part, Cherokee neither approached Linda nor retreated farther from her.

This went on for two or three minutes, after which Linda and Ashara engaged in a brief conversation that was too quiet to overhear in its entirety. What I did catch was Ashara's assurances to Linda that what had just taken place was perfect. It served as a reminder to Linda that she needed to check in with herself to make sure that she truly *was* standing in the round pen as a new person.

Turning her attention back to Cherokee, Linda walked over to him and stopped at his right side, up near his head. After pausing for a moment, she reached up and began stroking his face and neck. I watched as Cherokee accepted Linda's caresses without hesitation. He often had a momentary shy reaction to such intimate overtures by a new person, so I was delighted to see this, not only for Linda's sake, but for his as well.

I was grateful for the privilege of participating as a group member, for the valuable teaching I gleaned from Ashara's intuitive coaching process, and for the opportunity to see Cherokee show up so admirably as her partner. By the time Ashara brought things to a close, Cherokee had been separated from his herdmates for well over two hours because Bill had given Cherokee and me an especially long lesson immediately prior to the start of Linda's coaching session. So I was pleased that he had remained calm the whole time he was in the round pen with Linda.

The session was a beautiful demonstration of how the brick wall of our limiting beliefs could be dismantled and disposed of when readiness met opportunity. Linda had been ready, and Ashara, Cherokee, and a few props—human and otherwise— had provided an opportunity for Linda to bring to the surface and release some of her unfinished business.

Dahli Lama and Linda

A few months after Linda's coaching session with Cherokee and Ashara, she returned for a private, one-on-one session with me. I partnered with Dahli Lama, who was already out in the round pen. As Linda and I sat together, we practiced presence by connecting to our senses and releasing the circling thoughts as they arose in mind. When we opened our eyes, we could see that Dahli Lama was nibbling on the sparse pickings of grass just inside the rail that was closest to our chairs.

Linda picked a card from the wisdom deck I held and read the message aloud. It was replete with phrases like "taking the next step," "stepping into your power," and "walking forward in your power." We spoke briefly and then I invited her to go into the round pen after she had confirmed that she was comfortable going in there with such a young mare. It wouldn't have served anyone if an energy of fearfulness accompanied her through the gate. She walked to the center of the ring and took a minute to settle.

At two and a half years of age, Dahli Lama was not only still quite young, but she was also extremely inquisitive. And up to this point, she'd had very limited experience being enclosed in the round pen with someone she hadn't previously met. While the two of us had shared several colorful adventures since our first chakra meeting a year and a half earlier, this would be her first time partnering with me for an equine coaching session. I was curious to see what would unfold. At the same time, I knew I had to pay close attention to her movements, behavior, and attitude.

Dahli Lama immediately approached Linda and stopped directly in front of her. The mare's body language and manner exuded nonthreatening curiosity. I asked Linda to walk around the inside perimeter of the corral while observing what thoughts, if any, bubbled up about the message she'd read from her card. Dahli Lama followed her out to the rails and accompanied her around the pen, staying just off Linda's inside shoulder.

Interestingly, a few times Dahli Lama slowed down, placing her in a position of following close *behind* Linda rather than just off her shoulder. That resulted in her nose facing directly at the midsection of Linda's back. Even without any physical contact, that new alignment of their bodies had the effect of propelling Linda to move with noticeably more energy. Once or twice, Dahli Lama even made actual contact, gently pressing her muzzle into Linda's torso. Watching closely, I could see that Linda was fine with this behavior and, in fact, she chuckled as she walked along. She understood what was taking place. We both did.

After the two of them had made a full rotation or two, Dahli Lama stopped walking. Linda continued circling the perimeter, and as she walked, she spoke about wanting to work at what she loved and wanting to figure out what her equine coaching niche ought to be. And that was precisely when Dahli Lama walked back over to her and resumed walking alongside her.

The final offering from my equine partner came when Linda was standing back in the center of the round pen. Not surprisingly, Dahli Lama quickly joined her. But then things took a curious turn. Dahli Lama began actively sniffing and soft-nibbling various areas of Linda's body, and also engaged in leaching behavior by making certain mouth and lip movements.

Like me and other TBAH students, Linda was learning about the chakras in both equine and human bodies, the ability of horses to perform chakric alignments, and leaching behavior. It was evident, in watching the two of them interact, that Linda felt safe. She did, however, redirect the youngster a couple of times. Other than that, she stood in quiet receptivity.

Most of Dahli Lama's leaching was connected to the close attention she was paying to Linda's neck and shoulder areas, especially the left side, to which she returned a number of times. The sight of such intentionality and purposefulness was remarkable. Neither Linda nor I said a word throughout this process. After several minutes, Dahli Lama moved a few feet away. Clearly, she was finished with her ministrations. Like most other horses, Dahli Lama was not subtle about letting you know when she wished to bring her interactions with humans to a close.

I asked Linda to take a few moments before rejoining me to thank Dahli Lama for her participation and caretaking. Then, as we sat across from one another, Linda recounted her experiences in the round pen. Regarding the earlier part of the session, she had several valuable takeaways to report. She told me that Dahli Lama's nudges to her back made perfect sense to her, not only in light of the wisdom card she'd pulled but also because she was at a number of personal and professional crossroads in her life and was experiencing a lack of clarity and focus about which directions to take. I had never before known Dahli Lama to get behind me or anyone else in that fashion, and we agreed that Dahli Lama's actions had been deliberate and exactly what Linda needed in the moment.

As for the latter part of the session, Linda said that while she was standing in the center with Dahli Lama moving around her, she knew she was receiving a healing and that she could fully trust and embrace the way it was being offered. It was deeply gratifying to hear Linda confirm what my eyes had already shown me.

But there was a delightful postscript to the session. Linda had an appointment with her chiropractor the next day because her left shoulder region had been acting up. But sitting there, as the sun descended over the hogbacks just west of us, Linda wondered aloud whether she still needed to go for those adjustments.

I could imagine her telephone conversation with that medical office.

"Hi, this is Linda. I'm calling to cancel my appointment for tomorrow."

"No problem. Would you like to reschedule now or call back when you know which day would work better for you?"

"Well, actually, I don't think I'll be needing the shoulder adjustments after all. Earlier today, a horse did some energy work on me, right in that area, and it seems to have done the trick."

Dahli Lama and Diane

Equine coaching sessions can be deeply profound, but that doesn't mean they are all seriousness and hard effort. Humor frequently comes into play too.

And humor definitely played a part in Dahli Lama's session with my client, Diane. I was working with three women that day. Once we were all seated in our sacred circle and I had offered an opening dedication, I listened as the three women shared a little about themselves. Then they each selected a card from the *Whispers from a Horse's Heart* card deck and read them silently before taking turns briefly speaking to what stood out for them in their messages.

Diane, who had pulled the Partnership card from the deck, volunteered to do her coaching piece first and entered the round pen. From her introductory remarks, it was obvious that she was an upbeat, high energy kind of gal. Unprompted by me, she started running backward with a lively giddyap energy while encouraging Dahli Lama to pursue her. The filly took the bait and began following her around the inside perimeter of the corral. Diane had to maintain a fairly brisk pace to keep ahead of her equine counterpart.

At some point in this enterprise, Diane stumbled and fell backward to the ground. Dahli Lama reached her quickly and stood there, hovering over and staring down at her. For her part, Diane remained flat on her back and broke into full-throated laughter. After several seconds, she hoisted herself up on both elbows, lifted her head, and exclaimed, "Ha! I guess I had to literally ground myself so I could really get the message about partnership!"

I invited Diane to thank Dahli Lama for her participation and rejoin us in the circle. Fortunately, Diane was physically unhurt, and she was in good shape emotionally as well. In fact, she was downright giddy as she took her seat. One might conclude, reasonably enough, that while long on humor, that piece of work had been somewhat short on depth. But Diane had been quite impacted by the experience. While she had been able to see the humor in it, she also admitted the need to look more closely at the issue of partnership. Specifically, she recognized that it was important for her to examine why she tended to orchestrate her life along independent channels. The card she'd drawn had significance to her, and her work with Dahli Lama had grounded both her and the message.

When Diane was done speaking, I shared with everyone something that Melisa Pearce had said to a group of us during a training core. "You never forget the lesson from a thousand-pound horse." The women loved that, and we ended the session on that humorous and wise note.

Sometimes we have to learn our lessons in literal—and humorous—ways.

Saint and Hannah

Especially in the early going, some of my coaching sessions at the farmhouse weren't "official" ones in that they hadn't been planned, weren't for profit, and didn't involve sacred circles, wisdom cards, or other aids. Sometimes people showed up for a visit, having no coaching agenda in mind, and I simply took advantage of the opportunity to see if they wanted to go into the round pen and spend some time with one of the horses.

One January day, my daughter, Hannah, came to visit, and I asked her if she was up for going into the ring with Saint. I was curious to see how my somewhat undemonstrative fellow would respond because he hadn't yet partnered with me for any coaching pieces. Since Hannah wasn't a client, it wouldn't be a full-on coaching session, and while we were close, there was a good chance she might not feel wholly comfortable opening up about certain things that presented themselves. Still, not only would it be valuable for Saint to have the company and attention of another horse-loving person, it would also be good for Hannah since she no longer had many opportunities to hang out with horses. On top of this, it would give me a chance to see if Saint had any interest in the coaching work. I had faith that things would unfold as they were meant to.

Without any preliminary conversation or guidance, I had Hannah go into the round pen. Saint was already in there, searching for tidbits of the sparse winter grass. As I always did with clients, I asked Hannah to take a few minutes to become still in the center of the ring. Since she had a lot of practice with meditation and related practices in stillness, I let her do her own grounding. Next, I asked her to walk over to the rails and circumnavigate the inside perimeter of the round pen while observing—aloud or silently—what, if anything, was weighing on her heart.

Seated in my white plastic chair several feet from the ring, I watched as Saint followed Hannah out to the rails. They traveled in quiet tandem, Hannah having opted for inward contemplation. After a number of rotations, I asked her to cut into the center of the round pen. Saint followed her there, and when he came to a stop, he was facing her directly with his nose right up against her chest. It was such intimate and poignant behavior, not something he often displayed or offered.

After a few minutes, I asked Hannah if she thought Saint might be ready to rejoin his herdmates. Recalling a communication tool I'd learned in the equine coaching program, as well as from Bill Pelkey, I suggested that she ask Saint to blink if he wanted to do that. She did that, and sure enough, Saint not only blinked, he did so quite emphatically. Twice. Hannah immediately walked him over to the barnyard pasture where Dahli Lama and Cherokee were grazing and released him.

Later that afternoon, Hannah did some writing about the session and shared it with me the next day.

> Being in the ring with Saint, even for the very brief period of time, was an exquisite experience. I began simply by walking around the outer edge of the ring, thinking about some very meaningful things, including my hopes for the direction my life might take in the near future, as well as holding in my heart someone who meant a lot to me.
>
> When I was really fully connected to those feelings and right there with them, Saint made his way quietly up behind me, following me slowly but surely around the ring. Then I turned in toward the center, stopped, and grounded myself. And Saint was right there, stopped and waiting with me. After saying a few grateful words to him, I continued to walk around once more, and he followed closely behind when I returned to the center.

He started to chew and stick out his tongue and once again stood with me, head close to my face in the center. Although it was a short session, even that simple interaction actually brought tears behind my eyes as I stood with Saint, this great source of compassion and understanding.

When I read the part about the mouth and tongue movements that Hannah had noticed, I recognized them as releases on Saint's part. I had missed them completely and was grateful that she had not.

I was gladdened to read Hannah's description of her emotional experience with Saint that day. One thing was clear, both from reading her letter and observing her response to Saint's interactions with her: Being held in the pure compassion of a horse is no small thing.

Cherokee and Michael

When I was still a student in the TBAH program, the opportunity for a coaching session sometimes caught me off guard. That happened one morning when I was out in the round pen with Cherokee doing some groundwork. I didn't hear a car drive up or a car door slam, but I suddenly became aware of someone walking across the yard. I looked up and saw Michael, a friend from the coaching program. Without any social banter he asked, "Do you want to work with me?"

Taken by surprise, I nonetheless agreed to do it and came out of the round pen. There weren't even any chairs set out. It was just Michael, Cherokee, the round pen and me—and, of course, Colorado's trademark sunshine. I was a little nervous about the prospect of jumping into an impromptu coaching session like this. I also felt bad that I hadn't been able to explain to Cherokee what was happening before he was expected to partner with me for a piece of work. Still, I recognized that it would be an opportunity to honor the idea of working with a client without having even the slightest agenda in my mind or any possible props in the vicinity of the round pen.

Michael opened the round pen gate and walked a few feet inside. When he turned and faced me, I said nothing and did nothing. Rather than step into my role as coach, I stood there inert and waited for Michael to make the first move, assuming that he would simply guide himself through his own session. That was a foolish notion, though admittedly, Michael was senior to me in the program and a rather intense and somewhat brooding fellow.

He quickly sensed what was going on and called me out on it. "Aren't *you* going to participate?"

Busted and slightly embarrassed, I directed him to go into the center and quiet himself for a minute or so. Cherokee didn't join him there. No particular experiment or setup came to mind, so I invited Michael to walk over to the rails and circle around. Cherokee didn't choose to follow along with him, nor did he express much interest in our client.

I kept pace with Michael around the outside perimeter as he talked about his quandaries. On the few occasions when he stopped walking, I quietly reminded him to keep moving. All the while, I could see that while Cherokee was aware of Michael's presence and movements, he was still choosing not to travel around the ring with him. Instead, he meandered over to different spots, nibbling on the sparse late-winter grass offerings.

Michael wondered aloud. Should he settle down in Colorado where he had a sister living? Should he return to California? Was it the right time for him to be situated in a place where he could finally have his own horses? What kind of equine healing work would be a good fit for him? At some point, he began speaking about his recent experiences helping out on a few wilderness camp outings for young men. He really loved working with children, he said, and he thought he might have a talent for working with youth. But he quickly followed up his last remarks with a couple of self-denigrating ones.

That felt like the moment to interject. I asked him if he couldn't simply acknowledge his gifts. He didn't respond, but I could tell he'd heard my question. He continued walking a short distance, then he stopped and said, "I'm not honoring the universe by not obeying the messages I get." It was clear that he had dropped down from his head into an emotional space. He was facing me, and when I looked over at him, I saw that his eyes were moist.

My equine partner, too, had taken note of our client's altered state. When Michael first spoke about the wilderness outings, Cherokee had been standing clear across the corral. But by the time Michael fell silent, my gelding partner had crossed through and slightly beyond the center of the ring and stopped right at Michael's left side.

This stunning turnaround was the perfect place to bring the session to a close. Michael had just come to an important self-awareness, expressed with words. Cherokee then affirmed, with actions, the truthfulness and clarity he had picked up from Michael. They had each expressed their powerful sentiments in the language most natural for their respective species.

Michael's coaching piece had been a powerful demonstration of many lessons I was learning in the equine coaching program. One of these lessons was that horses can be counted on to resonate to the sound, vibration, and frequency of truth but show little if any interest in the false narratives that most of us humans tell ourselves all day long. Another lesson was that, as a student in the TBAH program, I needed to take every opportunity to put into practice what I was learning, even at those times when I felt unprepared or uncertain. Melisa was always impressing upon us the importance of simply showing up in the coaching work, come what may.

I had said yes to the opportunity the universe had presented to me that day, and my client ended up receiving an intuitive hit along those exact same lines. Now if that isn't serendipity and synchronicity at play, I don't know what is.

16

Magic Gained and Magic Lost

So much serendipity, synchronicity, and magic had come into my life with the writing of "Spirit Ride." Many significant events followed on the heels of writing that song: I was pulled to attend a horse retreat, met and deeply connected with a horse intended for riders more advanced than me, felt called to uproot my life and move across the country to live with that horse, and "stumbled across" an equine coaching program I enrolled in at once. How all of those events had unfolded felt mysterious and at the same time intentional. I knew I was living a blessed life.

Two more extremely meaningful and seminal events during that time were my selections, respectively, of the amulet bag and the horse fetish. So when I realized one day that both were missing, I felt deeply troubled. That particular unfolding event felt anything but magical or blessed.

I tried hard to recall the last time I'd seen or worn the amulet bag to no avail. As day after day of fruitless searching rolled out, sadness descended and cloaked me from heart to toe. For weeks, I couldn't walk across any of the rooms in my home without stopping to look for the amulet bag in a drawer, on a shelf, under a couch, or in every other place I'd already looked for it several times. Despondency proved all but impossible to shake. The disappearance felt like an emotional sucker punch. Perhaps the real potency of those objects, their animating force, came from the storehouse of memories they held. Regardless, a bit of magic was missing.

I'd mostly kept my despair about the situation to myself, but during a telephone conversation with my friend Danae, I expressed my grief about the missing talismans. It was such a relief finally to be sharing my despondency with a kindred spirit, someone who understood the depth of my woe. She listened sympathetically and then recited an exquisite affirmation whose words she attributed to American New Thought leader, Florence Scovel Shinn: "That which is mine cannot be lost to me. Infinite Spirit is never late. I joyfully receive that which is mine. I cannot lose it."

The words had a healing and cleansing effect, and I hung up with my spirits lifted. For weeks afterward, I repeated the affirmation both silently and aloud. The sincerity of my belief in the words made it a powerful mantric practice.

Shortly after my conversation with Danae, I came upon another quote that also helped me, that one from Rumi: "Do not grieve. Anything you lose comes 'round in another form."

It was a challenging time for me, though on the silver lining side of life, I did learn valuable lessons about the heavyhearted nature of attachment, the lighthearted nature of surrender, and the fullhearted nature of grace. My treasured talismans did not miraculously reappear, but I knew that serendipities, synchronicities, and magical connections being what they were, anything was possible. And after all, I found *reappear* to be a pretty slippery, shapeshifting sort of word.

A month or so later, I drove up to Pine Junction by myself, to spend a day with my friend Sharra at her place, which she named, "Paradise." That afternoon, we headed out for a hike with Deb, a friend of hers who had dropped by for a surprise visit. I made a comment about how wonderful it was that Sharra and her animals could share the beauty and privacy of that land, and Sharra, who had been walking slightly ahead of me, turned around to face me. With arms outstretched to take in all of mother nature, she exclaimed, "This or something better!"

I was struck by her words, coming as they did while we were already surrounded by such panoramic abundance. Still, her spontaneous affirmation, hurled out to the Universe, Spirit, God, Source—call it what you will—turned out to be quite prescient for both of us. Dramatic events manifested in both of our lives within a few weeks' time. In Sharra's case, the stars aligned for her dream of relocating to South America. She celebrated her seventieth birthday as a new resident of Ecuador, and within days of arrival, she found new love with a fellow American expat. As for me, I wasn't transported to another continent, but an event took place in Lyons, Colorado, soon after Sharra's departure that did take me on a remarkable inner journey.

One day I drove over to The Stone Cup in Lyons for breakfast, reading, and journaling, and afterward, something told me to stop at the Lyons recycling center to drop off some items I'd been driving around with for several days. Although I came into Lyons pretty regularly, I just felt compelled to make the deposits right then and there.

I pulled up beside the huge green bins and made two or three trips with my recyclables. As I was walking back to the car after the last load, my eye caught sight of a small grouping of items lying on the ground off to the side of one of the bins. I walked over to investigate and saw some footwear, a few books, a few more odds and ends, and one *very* surprising item: a horse figure about fifteen inches long, four inches wide, and ten inches high. I picked it up and saw that it was in excellent condition.

It wasn't a stuffed animal. Rather, the body was hollow and solid, and the four sturdy legs were made to be bent in various positions. The horse had light brown eyes and a light brown, slightly orange-tinged coat, velvety in texture. The tail and mane were both blonde, the face had a white blaze on the nose, and it had white socks on all four legs. *Four white socks, a white blaze and a light brown coat with a slightly orange hue.*

I stared at the horse for several seconds, astonished, because it bore an uncanny resemblance to Saint. I carried the horse back to the car, placed it on the front passenger seat, stroked its faux fur once, and drove home. Parked in the driveway, I made no move to get out. Instead, I began to sob. I sat there for some time, and after a while, Sharra's exuberant, "This or something better!" came to mind. I saw crazy-magical connections between how deeply that phrase had resonated with me at the time, my ongoing distress about the missing medicine pouch and fetish, and my discovery of that recycled horse. In that context, Sharra's words sounded like a veritable *demand* made to the Universe—a gauntlet thrown down.

I didn't want to diminish my attachment to the diminutive retreat fetish, but I had to admit that the oversized version bore a much stronger resemblance to the living and breathing Saint. While the retreat fetish did have the right body color and light brown eyes that were similar to Saint's, it had no white blaze, no blonde mane or tail, and no socks. The experience felt mystical and serendipitous.

It was also highly cathartic, allowing me to let go of an enormity of emotional baggage around my missing retreat fetish. The fullheartedness of grace was showing itself again— first with the release I had felt by continuously repeating those words of Francis Scovel Shinn and now with the release that my serendipitous trip to the recycling center had gifted me.

A few years later, I came across another translation of that same affirmation attributed to Florence Scovel Shinn. When I read it, the second line struck me as prophetic: "There is no loss in Divine Mind. Therefore, I cannot lose anything which belongs to me. It will be restored, or I will receive its equivalent."

At first blush, the disappearance of my horse fetish had felt like a wholly negative event. But then the recycling center discovery was made, and it was one of the most wondrous lessons in serendipity and magical connections I had ever experienced. That event made me reflect more deeply on the mysterious nature of the universe and Spirit and on those invisible threads that were weaving away, creating my unfolding life story. Could I live my life fully trusting that the universe—replete with its serendipities and disappointments, its happy circumstances and distressing ones—was no doubt unfolding as it should (as Max Ehrmann put it in "Desiderata")?

Even in its absence, that little horse figurine had exerted a strong influence on me in the form of all of those metaphysical and spiritual considerations.

17

Shapeshifting Relationships

W*atch the shape of things.* That message was seeping into so many nooks and crannies of my life.

On a trek in the snow with a friend, I'd felt an impulse to stop walking and sent my friend and her dog on ahead. I was being called to stillness and knew I needed to honor that call. I turned my gaze to the sun and clouds above and was treated to an astonishing sight. Swirling cloud movements were dancing across the huge, perfect roundness of the sun. I closed my eyes and watched a plethora of vibrant colors shapeshifting behind my closed eyelids. Then I sat down and slowly opened my eyes to take in the sparkling almost blinding whiteness before lying back and stretching out all four limbs to make a fallen angel.

Back on my feet, I began following the tracks my friend and her dog had made in the snow. Soon I was struck by the sight of two tall trees off to my left that stood about five or six feet apart. I turned to face and greet them, telling them how beautiful they were. I was especially attracted to their trunks and couldn't take my eyes away from that part of their beautiful bodies. I began to see animal images in the gorgeous textures of the bark, first in the tree to the left and then in the one to the right: the image of a horse, followed by that of a dog; a human eye; and two more animals, one of which was the original horse. Then several shapes began to appear as eyes, one after another.

In the midst of all of this eye imagery, I heard in mind a message that I knew came from the trees: *Watch the shape of things.* This wasn't the first time that phrase had come to mind since moving out West. As life filled up with horses, dogs, cats, and woodland adventures, I came to understand a few things about shapes and shapeshifting. One of those things was that, just as with objects in the physical realm, nonphysical things— thoughts, feelings, memories, somatic awarenesses, decisions, emotions—also had shapes that could be watched. Substantial shapes with form. And like anything else that comes into or passes out of being in consensual reality or elsewhere, their shapes could shift.

On another trek, that understanding crystalized even further. One wintry day, I headed out with Stitch and Billy for a long walk along the Highland Ditch. One of the real pleasures of outings along the ditch was that the dogs could be off leash since no one else had access to that fenced stretch of land.

Billy, especially, loved those outings. Being part hound, he was a slave to his olfactory sense. He would race ahead of us, lured by the wealth of scents that abounded. Stitch, on the other hand, was more concerned about my whereabouts than the sources of those aromas and would only walk a short distance ahead of me. Even then, he would turn his head back regularly to make sure I hadn't disappeared.

I had adopted Stitch when he was two years old, and shortly before he turned six, he became afflicted with a condition that consumed me to an extent more readily conveyed in tears than in words: degenerative myelopathy, an incurable progressive disease of the spinal cord. I quickly learned that veterinarian neurologist, Roger Clemmons, was the premier expert on the disease, and I not only adopted all of his dietary guidelines, I also put in place other protocols, including additional supplements, Reiki, and prayer.

Although I read numerous articles, clinical trial results, and chat room testimonials, I also practiced self-care by eschewing all the scariest parts of the online material. I was determined to do whatever I could, and then some, to stave off the onset of paralysis. Thankfully, Stitch stayed ambulatory and content. Another saving grace was that the condition was not a painful one, and Stitch continued to adore our walks.

Whenever we headed out on the Highland Ditch trail, both boys loved climbing down to the shallow stream. There were several places where the slope was gradual enough for the dogs to access the water, and for a time, Stitch was able to make the descent in each of these spots. But eventually, I had to take care to invite him to go down in only two or three of them. In that way, I would set us both up for success in meeting the challenges of our respective terrains—Stitch's physical and mine emotional—and we both got what we needed.

When we were heading back home that day, I decided that the three of us should take a shorter route by cutting across the west pasture. The boys went under the fence as I held the bottom wire up to give them as much clearance as possible, and then I climbed over the top. Roughly midway between the northern and southern borders of that field, there was a gradual, fairly steep ridge that spanned nearly the entire width of the pasture. In getting back down to the barn and beyond, we had to navigate that descent.

As we approached the ridge, both dogs trotted ahead of me. I found myself focused on Stitch and how he would handle the slope in his condition. But I wasn't just *thinking*. I was engaging in a philosophical sort of exchange with myself.

Thought: *Oh, no. How will he handle the slope with his condition?*

Awareness: *I need to dismiss the negative energy of that question.*

Thought: *Well, this is a good opportunity for him to be able to achieve this descent, even with his condition.*

Awareness: *This is just another limiting idea, albeit one seemingly more attractive in outlook and perspective.*

Thought: *Let me just simply watch him, just watch him as a dog walking ahead of me.*

After a few liberating moments of watching Stitch in that not-quite-but-close-to-neutral way and also taking note of the way my thoughts had just unfolded, I recalled the powerful message the twin trees had sent me: *Watch the shape of things.* There it was again. I wondered what I needed to learn.

By the time I reached the ridge, I was still some distance behind Stitch, who was already making his descent. Just before starting to make my own, I looked down at the ground and saw a magnificent stone. It was quite large, roughly six inches by six inches, with many edges and crevices that flashed with silver and grey flecks. I was enchanted and picked it up. As I ran my hand over its many wonderful surfaces, I knew it had to come home with us.

Immediately, I saw serendipity and meaning in the timing at play. That big rock would serve to remind me to release any limiting ideas about Stitch. I realized that the best thing I could do was hold him in a neutral light, eschewing such limiting ideas as, *he's walking well today, he's struggling today, he looks better today,* or *he looks worse today.* In that way, I would be offering him the most propitious energy medicine possible as we continued our journey through his affliction. I dubbed the rock my "energy stone reminder."

✳

Not only was the shape of things changing in my relationship with Stitch, it was also changing in my relationships with my equine relatives. Certainly, my individual relationships with each of the horses had been evolving as time went on. But a shift of a greater and more encompassing magnitude was also taking place. It was a transformation in what it meant to me to be a member of a horse and human herd. And in its enormity, it informed not only how I saw myself in relation to Cherokee, Saint, and Dahli Lama but also to The Horse in a collective sense.

In the months preceding the move to Colorado, I saw myself as someone who was moving out West to live with a horse (Cherokee) and take rides on him hither and yon. I cherished my memories of the twice-daily rides on Cherokee at the retreat. That self-image held steady for the first couple of years in Longmont. In fact, for the first year or so of my groundwork and riding lessons with Bill, I had been a dedicated and enthused client, though sometimes overthinking and despairing got the better of me during our lessons.

But my self-image and the intentions undergirding it morphed dramatically, and once they did, the trajectory of my joined journey with the herd was forever altered. What arose in its place was a kind of spiritual imperative that could neither be ignored nor dismissed.

The truth was that there came a time when I started seriously questioning whether or not I wanted to ride my own horses or anyone else's horses. I struggled with the quandary of imposing my will on my horses in that particular way. I knew that throughout the world, there were many riding partnerships that were deeply rewarding for equine and human alike. But I had the dawning recognition that my purposes in coming west had much more to do with deepening the capacity to explore inner pathways than mastering the capacity to navigate horse trails. *That* was the clarion call I had heeded.

I never shared those quandaries and realizations with Bill. Instead, I continued to train with him. I also didn't share my dilemma with anyone else. Nearly everyone I befriended in Colorado was a horse person. Most of them rode horses, took lessons to learn how to ride, or intended to take up riding again someday. And virtually all of them held either cherished memories of horses ridden in the past or hopeful dreams of riding them in the future. I didn't know anyone whose life was shaped liked mine—that is, anyone who lived alone with horses and who was seriously considering giving up riding them (though physically able to do so) but was still happily committed to bearing sole responsibility for their upkeep and welfare for the rest of their lives.

And so it was that, well before my riding came to an abrupt halt in late April of 2014, my self-image as a horsewoman had already been shapeshifting for some time. Fate intervened that April day.

I decided to try something new with Cherokee that day and see where it took us. After lunging and free-schooling Cherokee in the round pen, I would mount him. We would travel several rotations, including a couple of figure eights through the center. We would maintain a walking gait for the most part, but I would also ask him to move up to the trot and come back down to the walk several times to assess how well he was responding to my cues for him to change back and forth between the two gaits.

Assuming he responded willingly and reliably to my requests and cues, I would ask him to walk us back out of the ring, turn to his left, and take us about eight to ten yards away. Once we arrived at a spot that felt right, I would dismount, offer generous praise, and then release him. End of session.

Normally, I closed the round pen gate behind me when I worked with one of the horses inside the round pen, but that day I had purposely left it open. Since I hadn't yet learned how to ask a horse to side pass, I wouldn't have been able to get close enough to the gate latch while remaining mounted.

Cherokee did really well during our rotations and figure eights, so the next phase of the plan was still a go. He took us through the gate and walked us a short distance to our left, all the while maintaining a nice calm walk. I brought him to a halt and stroked the left side of his neck as I said, "Good boy. Good boy." All that was left to do was dismount, offer praise and a few treats, remove the saddle, blanket, and side pull bridle, and walk away well satisfied. But just then, something that was decidedly *not* part of the agenda happened and stopped me from dismounting.

The something was Dahli Lama. Throughout the session with Cherokee, she had been grazing in the barnyard that surrounded the round pen, but at a distance from us. I realized in hindsight—brilliant, perfectly coiffed hindsight—that it hadn't been a smart idea to execute this first-time agenda while Dahli Lama was loose in that same field, let alone without having Bill on hand.

No sooner had I brought Cherokee to a halt and praised him than I spotted Dahli Lama just off to our left. She came over and walked right up to Cherokee's nose. Their meeting was quiet and calm, at least from my human perspective. As I watched the two of them sniffing each other, I considered my next move. Normally, I would dismount on Cherokee's near side, the usual side for getting off a horse. But if I did that, I would be doing so while sandwiched snugly between the two horses. That didn't seem like a safe move, so I ruled it out. I thought about dismounting on his off side, but not only would that maneuver likely feel odd and possibly unsettling to Cherokee, it would also be a first for me. So that idea, too, was quickly dismissed. That whole chain of thoughts occurred within seconds.

Before I came up with an answer, Cherokee abruptly took off to our left. He started off with an immense burst of energy and picked up speed from there. In no time at all, we were moving at a gallop across the wide yard, and I panicked.

It was Rabbit Mountain all over again, only at a gallop.

Both reins had way too much slack in them, and once again, my hands were completely out of position. Also, both of my arms were raised up high rather than down low at my hips. It didn't occur to me to slide one of my hands down the rein to bring Cherokee's head around and slow our velocity. I couldn't think straight, and my energy was a sickly mix of disbelief and terror.

I managed to keep my seat while we were on a straight-away, but we were approaching the large, fenced dog kennel that curved around the southern side of the house. There was only about ten feet between the kennel fence and the fence enclosing the property. As we careened around the curve, I flew off of Cherokee and both felt and heard the sound of the thud as I hit the ground. Flat on my back on the ground, stunned but conscious, I had enough wits about me to consider that I probably shouldn't try to move. Still, I couldn't resist the urge to see if my body had *any* capacity to do so. I shifted my body the tiniest bit and then immediately hoped I hadn't done any further damage.

The horses were nowhere in sight, and other than Billy and Stitch, who were staring at me from their side of the kennel fence, I was alone. Because it was late in the afternoon on a Saturday, my landlord's ranch hands were probably already gone. Had they passed by in their trucks just then, they would surely have spotted me, since I was only a foot or so from the fence they had to drive by on their way out.

Fortunately, I had obeyed Elizabeth's and Hannah's insistence that I never ride the horses without my phone. The hip pouch that held the phone had come undone and was lying a few feet from me. I didn't relish the idea of risking further physical movement, but knew I had no choice. I needed to call for help. Slowly inching one of my legs over to the pouch, I managed to nudge it back to me.

I called Kim, my friend from the equine coaching program, who lived in another section of Longmont. She was also a registered nurse with over twenty years of experience. Thankfully, she answered the phone, and I stammered three staccato words to her: "Fell. Horse. Come." Before long, I heard a car pull up and turned my head enough to see Kim running over to me. She ordered me to not move and called for an ambulance.

That she had even been home when I called her was serendipitous. Earlier that day, she had called the hospital she worked at and took herself off the schedule for the night shift because she had decided to drive to the barn to spend some time with her two horses. But then, at the last minute, she changed her mind and decided to stay home.

Later that night, Kim told me that once the paramedics had immobilized my neck, placed me on a backboard, and secured me inside the ambulance, she had walked across the property and approached Cherokee. He was standing alone and still had the saddle attached to him. It had loosened and swiveled all the way around, hanging down in what must have been a very unsettling position for him. Fortunately, he was physically uninjured, though he was probably mentally and emotionally affected by our misadventure. She removed the saddle and other tack and then drove over to the hospital. She also called Hannah, who drove down from Breckenridge.

I wasn't as lucky as Cherokee and sustained a few injuries:

a fractured left scapula, fractures of several vertebrae, and a cracked rib. By grace, none of those injuries required surgical intervention, a brace, or even an extended hospital stay. I was discharged into Hannah's care after a day and a half. She stayed with me for the next five days, after which Luis flew in from New York and took care of me for the following five. Although I had hurt him terribly, we had remained on very good terms, and all of my family visits back East included him.

My body's healing process was swift, just a few weeks. Once I was home from the hospital, what was most important to me was being able to tell Cherokee, *in person*, that I was fine, that it wasn't his fault, that I didn't blame him in any way, and that I loved him dearly. The first day I could manage it, I walked slowly and gingerly out to the barn and did just that.

As I watched the shape of my thoughts and feelings during that time, I saw clearly that I'd lost all desire to be carried on the backs of any of my horses, though I continued to be physically fit to do so. That chapter of my life with the herd was over. What I really wanted to devote myself to was deepening my capacity to communicate with them and gaining more experience partnering with them in my budding equine coaching career.

These awarenesses didn't arise out of fearfulness but from finally admitting something to myself I had known intuitively for some time: that the satisfaction I derived from a horseback ride paled in comparison to the peace I felt when interacting with the horses from the ground. My deepest sense of kinship with the herd came while grooming, hugging, sharing breath with, and talking with them, and also while partnering with them during coaching sessions.

The accident had simply offered me the opportunity to finally honor the rumblings that had been pointing me toward certain truths: The skills I really wanted to master with my herd didn't have anything to do with riding. They had to do with becoming the best caretaker and guardian of the horses, learning how to communicate with them through telepathic and other energetic channels, and discovering who they were as individual souls.

I had already gained a deeper understanding of my relationship with Cherokee, recognizing that he was an archetypal presence in my life, a representational figure who was there to teach me the value of hearing, trusting, and heeding the wordless yet cogent messages that stir the heart. In connection with this deeper understanding of our bond, I had intuited a mystical connection between writing my song, "Spirit Ride," meeting Cherokee soon after, and then sharing with him all those experiences that ultimately brought me westward. I sensed that the genesis of that song was rooted in something beyond the confines of my personal history and that the lyrics had come through so effortlessly because I had tapped in to an archetypal energy field. The seeds of my joined journey with Cherokee had been planted with the channeling of that song, and perhaps even earlier.

There were also important shifts in my relationships with all the other animal relatives with whom I was living. Most importantly, though, my relationship with myself had gradually morphed. I had become a woman who trusted the knowledge that came through intuitively, telepathically, somatically, and otherwise more deeply than ever before.

I was grateful for this shift in my self-identity because it helped me to better understand why I felt called to live with so many animals and what my purpose was in coming into their lives and bringing them into mine. One ability I knew I needed to better develop was how to handle their mortality. It wasn't enough to experience the joy and sacredness of life with my animal relatives while they were enjoying full and healthy lives. I needed to continue to deepen my capacity to stay strong during their times of transition. Like everyone else who had endured those rites of passage, I was doing my best, but I knew that life—and death—would give me more opportunities to hone that capacity.

18

The Hardest Part of the Journey

I am either the best or the worst kind of person to have pets. The best because I always strive to do my utmost for them and because I respect their embodiments as having as much intrinsic value as those of humans; the worst because of the emotional toll it takes on me when one of them falls ill, is injured, shows any signs of being in pain, or needs me to let them go. Actually, I am probably both or neither.

I've had several animal relatives die during my adult life, and most of those deaths have been the result of a conscious decision on my part. Once I knew, deep down in my soul-bones, that it was time to set them free, I honored my duty to them by making that painful decision. With some of the losses, I felt I might never get over the grief, might never again know happiness. Yet somehow, with the presence of grace and the passage of time, my bruised heart began to heal. Always, I have been both grateful and relieved when the agony softened, transformed into the peace and comfort that came from knowing I had done the compassionate thing. Mercy shown and mercy received. Another full circle to acknowledge.

I've reflected upon what goes on in my being when I am face-to-face with that sacred duty, and I can see that several personas show up. Logical Nancy is capable of objectively and unsentimentally assessing the situation, at least in short spurts. Frantic Nancy rails against having to make the decision, plea-bargaining with God: *Please, please, if he/she can recover from this and stay with me a while longer, I promise I'll never complain about anything else for the rest of my life.* Dissociating Nancy wants desperately to dull herself to the whole situation and escape the inescapable. She longs to jump in the car and head over to her favorite coffeehouse, where she can vanish into a book, a video, or her journal. Any alternative reality will do.

During these heartbreaking rites of passage, it is as if everything I've ever believed about God, Atman, the Self, Source, Spirit, reincarnation, or the life-death-life cycle holds no sway—despite decades of philosophical, spiritual, and meditative pursuits. When they're in good health and spirits, of course, it's much easier to avoid confronting this lack of a spiritual spine. But each time I even suspect that the time has come for any of my cherished animal relatives to cross over, the words of the wise can't be heard all that well over the loud thumping of my heart.

But there is another Nancy who makes an appearance: Brave Nancy. For the sake of her beloved, Brave Nancy sighs, does not weep, takes deep breaths as needed, sits quietly with her departing relative, thanks him or her for being such wonderful company for so long, and offers sincere reassurances that it is okay to go, that she will be fine. I persevere in this courageousness as things unfold, keeping my commitment to bear witness and be good company right up to the final moments when the veterinarian inserts the first needle, rendering the animal unconscious, and then the second one, stopping the heart.

Throughout the event, I take care to fix my eyes on one or both of the eyes of my beloved one, watching as the light of consciousness literally goes out of them. Eyes that moments before were shining with liquid life are now dulled by the lack of life force. I know, then, that the soul of yet another of my cherished companions has been freed from their spent body. It feels important to me to bear witness to the transition. Though I cannot fully articulate why this is so, I honor the imperative without question. Perhaps there is within me an intuitive belief that a joined journey travels its fullest measure when one companion takes leave of its body while held in the presence of the other.

I am grateful that my capacity to love and be loved by the rest of my animal relatives remains intact despite the losses that come my way. It's not magic. It's a matter of just waking up the morning after the loss and greeting the furry companions who are still alive and with me. One look into their eyes and there I am, opening the can of cat food, dicing the apple, or tossing the stick to be fetched.

True, my capacity to feel the pain of these losses also remains intact. There will be other losses, equine and otherwise, and as much as I might like to hold fast to the capacity to love and take a hard pass on the capacity to feel the pain, I know that this is probably not how the rest of my journey through mortality and loss is likely to go. And that's okay, for I do believe that come what may, an open heart is a blessing, not a curse. Living my life in this belief aligns with my deepest understandings about why I have been given the gift of a human embodiment. And there is always the hope that another capacity continues to evolve within my soul—that of integrating more deeply and resoundingly the belief in the life-death-life cycle.

As I contemplated such matters as life, death, love, and loss while sitting in a hot tub in Breckenridge, Colorado, I wrote a poem. Luckily, I had brought a pen and notebook with me and had them within arm's reach.

If I Should Die Tomorrow

If I should die tomorrow,
I have deeply seen the trees,
Spoken to the rock folks,
Felt grounded in the listening.
And my angels waited so patiently.
If I should die tomorrow,
I have heard mantric beats of "All is Well,"
Known the grace of doubtlessness,
Cried countless tears to the Mysteries.
If I should die tomorrow,
I have seen "question-and-answer mind" fall away,
And tasted gratitude for those fleeting moments of glory.
If I should die tomorrow,
I have shared my wonder with others,
Rejoiced in their slightest gladness,
Known the Oneness of All-many times, in truth;
And forgiven myself the forgetting:
Yes, forgiven myself the forgetting!

Gratitude, forgiveness, the will to go on:
I bow to Spirit for these graces.
And for each moment that only stillness remains,
That greatest grace is Om.

Saint's First Parting Gift

On October 10, 2015, Saint colicked. I was miserable and scared as I watched him go through it. Unlike the other two colic episodes he'd suffered in the past year, this one was full-fledged and relentless, showing no signs of easing up. For several hours, there hadn't been any gut sounds on either side of his body and no urinating, pooping, or passing gas. There also had been no eye contact or desire to engage with me, his mates, or his surroundings.

All of this was evidence of pain and distress, which in all likelihood was obvious to Bill and to Laurie, the veterinarian. It was obvious to me as well, at least in those fleeting moments when denial was overcome by the reality of what my eyes were seeing and my gut was registering. Still, neither Bill nor Laurie did or said anything to sway my decision. They respected that it was mine and mine alone to make. It must have been hard for Bill, in particular, to watch me navigate my way through the turmoil.

The decision-making process was quietly excruciating. At some point, I remembered a message that had come to me while I was alone with Saint a few years earlier. We had been standing together in the round pen, and while thinking about his calm and steady nature, I had a flash of insight: Saint's main contribution as a coaching partner would be to allow people to stand without fear. That phrase, *stand without fear*, was an offering from Spirit. At the time, I understood the message to mean that he would empower people not only to conquer their fear of horses but also to face life's challenges uncrippled by fear.

Standing there with Saint as he endured what was to be his final bout with colic, I understood something else about that round pen message, something I couldn't possibly have known back then: His contribution was destined to help not just our clients but me. He would help *me* find the courage to stand without fear. Not fear of horses or fear of life, but fear of death, specifically *his* death. Once again, the generosity and grace of serendipity dropped me to my spiritual knees.

When the moments of clarity became less fleeting and denial less possible, I was ready to honor my sacred duty as Saint's human guardian. It was incumbent upon me to spare him any further suffering. I needed to let him go. I told Laurie, who'd been so patient throughout the long afternoon, that I'd made the decision to let Saint cross over. She agreed to carry out the procedure then and there, so I called Bill, who had left fifteen minutes earlier. He turned around and headed right back to the farm.

Meanwhile, I walked Saint over to his favorite pasture, the one directly in front of the house, and stood silently with him while Laurie opened up the back of her truck and started preparing the necessary medicines. At one point, she turned to me and softly said, "If you'd like to go into the house while everything is taken care of, this would be a good time to do that."

"Thank you, really, but no," I said quietly, making an effort to stay composed, mainly for her sake. "I need to be here. I need to stand with him, bear witness, you know? But thank you for asking. Thank you."

Tears filled my eyes as I watched Laurie turn back to her task. Bill's car pulled up and he joined us at the far end of the pasture. He kissed my cheek, hugged me briefly, then walked over to Saint's right side. He spoke softly to him at some length while also making subtle gestures with his right hand on Saint's neck. When Bill stepped away, I walked around to Saint's left side and told him how much he was adored. I also thanked him for the blessing of his extraordinary presence in my life.

As Laurie administered the first injection, I chanted a Sanskrit prayer sometimes referred to as "The Perfect Prayer." It was hard to get some of the words up from my choked-up throat, but in the end, they were all sounded. I was at the mercy of the gods, and they had chosen to grace me with all the emotional strength I needed for the task.

It is not easy to watch a horse go down. You stand there, helpless to take away *their* helplessness. Once the drugs they have been injected with begin to take effect, their legs grow wobbly. Instinctively, they fight, albeit briefly, to regain their footing, their firm hold on the earth, their ability to flee perceived threats. But failing in that, their legs give way and they collapse to the ground. The too-awful thud that a horse's massive head makes when it hits the hard earth is a legacy that stays with you forever and a day—because that is what legacies are supposed to do.

Still, on the day of Saint's passing, that generous measure of grace kept me upright and strong enough all the way through, enabling me to stay present as Saint's spirit left his body. I watched the light of consciousness literally go out from his left eye, the eye that was visible to me as he lay on the ground.

Afterward, as Bill walked me back toward the house, he told me that during his communion with Saint, he had recited sacred Japanese words that represented Reiki power symbols and had also "drawn" them on Saint's body with his finger. Then, without my asking, he said that I had made the right decision, that Saint had conveyed to him that it was time for him to go. I was deeply grateful to Bill, not only for his farewell blessing to Saint but also for passing along to me that reassuring message.

Saint's final gift to me, while still alive, had been the opportunity for me to stand without fear as I made and carried out the decision to let his soul fly free of a worn-out body and, from a larger perspective, to show bravery in the face of a decades-long (or lifetimes-long) distress around mortality and its nonnegotiable finality.

I didn't fail either him or myself. Though I never quite shook the feeling that I had been asked to hasten the coming of the worst of all losses, I kept going and played my part as best I could. This was *my* gift to *him* on this final day of our joined journey in the physical realm.

Saint's Second Parting Gift

A week after his passing, Saint gave me a second parting gift, this time from beyond the veil. It was an extraordinary exchange with a soul freed of embodiment and rich with visions, somatic awarenesses, and intelligible messages. The clairsentient and telepathic quality of it was undeniable—so much so that I was left with no sabotaging doubts from any would-be naysaying inhabitants of my brain.

After the experience was over, I sat there quietly for a short while before getting up to retrieve my journal from my back-pack. Needing to be undistracted by Billy's and Stitch's adoring but demanding eyes as I wrote, I retreated to a quiet room.

Tears arose in the kitchen tonight while I was straightening up the kitchen after feeding the dogs. They seemed to have arisen from out of nowhere, seemingly not preceded by a causal thought. I stopped and stood still in front of the sink, sobbing, and had the thought that the tears had to do with Saint, were about Saint. I was moved to go into the bathroom to be alone with myself and whatever was taking place within me. I closed the door so the dogs couldn't have access to me.

I kept the light off and sat down in the dark on the toilet seat, my hands clasped together. As the sobbing continued, I began talking to Saint. The words fell out in sentence fragments. "Your soft eyes and how intently you sometimes looked at me with those eyes. Your golden fetlock, mane and tail. How much we softened together, and how much I loved hugging your neck and putting my face close to yours. How much I loved cleaning poop from your legs. I would've gladly washed your legs for another twenty years if you'd had a healthy body and had been content to stay alive. I miss you, Saint. I love you so much."

Then I asked, "Do you have a message for me?" I didn't
hear or otherwise receive anything that I recognized as
a message. I didn't wait long before asking him another
question. "Are you well?" An inner commentary of
a slightly critical nature arose about how it wasn't
useful to bombard the horse with whom you're trying
to communicate with multiple questions. So I asked,
"Can you give me a sign that you're hearing me?"
I sat there, my body very still—rock-like. At some
point, the sobbing had subsided and I was just sitting
there, waiting behind closed eyes, continuing to do my
best to surrender the yearning, the conjuring efforts,
the machinations of monkey *manas*, in a sincere effort
to endeavor just to *be* with whatever was presenting
itself, and even less / more than this: just to *be*. It wasn't
easy. Still, the heart was willing, and at least some of
the mental chatter abated.
During that expanse of time, no images of Saint
arose in mind, either of their own accord or through
conjuration. Still, I waited. Then I asked him again,
"Can you give me a sign that you're hearing me?" I
was aware of how deeply I was longing to have him
show himself.
After a while longer, I was suddenly in tears again and
was also overtaken by a kind of. . .glowing. A kind of
inner and outer glowing. It wasn't an experience of
a bright light being *seen* before my closed eyes, nor
was it a sensation of warmth or heat being *felt* within.
It was more an infusion of presence—a *knowing* that

Saint was present. I knew I was with him and he was with me.

It was a very intense experience, not merely because of the wellspring of emotion coursing through me, or the sobbing, or even how completely different that glow was from anything I'd ever experienced. The intensity stemmed from how real Saint's presence was, and also from my awareness that I was experiencing some fearfulness about what was happening.

That infusion of presence—Saint's—was nearly overwhelming. It went on for some time, during which I was moved to say aloud, "Okay, all right," a few times. I sat there sobbing and experiencing that "glowing knowing."

I still didn't see any images of Saint in my mind. But then I heard the phrase "stand without fear" and had a flash of understanding: Saint was giving me a message that I needed to stand without fear of those kinds of communications. As that was going on, it was profoundly clear to me that we were truly in each other's company.

At some point, I knew, deep down in my soul bones, that the tears accompanying the expanding infusion, the glowing presence, was Saint presenting himself to me, not in the form of any images of him or his scent or his words, but in the form of those tears and that glowing sense of his presence, which was at once within and without.

After a while, I started to experience a sense of worry,

of lament, along the lines of *this present experience of being with Saint is going to come to an end, and when will I have the next experience of being with him*?

I tried to quell the low but undeniable level of angst that it was producing to allow myself to stay with Saint in the here and now for as long as possible. The desire to stay there with him was *so* pronounced. As I sat there, still teary, I became aware of a kind of fading of the experience of the glow, and it was understood that Saint was starting to withdraw his presence, to take his leave of me. After his presence was no longer palpable, no longer being felt through that glowing portal, I wasn't left with any sort of grieving that he had left me for good.

Instead, I continued to sit there, eyes and nose still leaking, awash in some sort of emotional afterglow that I couldn't quite put my finger on, beyond saying that the state was also very intense, though in a quieter sort of way. I had been with Saint and was not yet ready for physical movement or return to the world of Stitch, Billy, and activities beyond the union with which I'd just been graced. So I allowed myself to sit a short while longer, sniffing, sighing, and dabbing my eyes with the nearby hand towel.

Then I was ready—or, at least, a little readier—to move back into the world at large. I stood up, opened the bathroom door, and silently greeted my beloved canines, who were lying there, faithfully awaiting my return to them. I carried my dinner upstairs to the bedroom, turned on the light, and set the bowl down. There, waiting for me, was the large Saint fetish standing on the dresser. I stroked its nose, adjusted its fetlock, and planted a gentle kiss.

When I think of Saint, it is one particular scenario that usually comes to mind. Appropriately enough, it has to do with treats. In my mind's eye, I see a moving picture of a sweet ritual that had developed between the two of us during the last year or so of his life. I return home from wherever I've been and park the car. As I cut the engine, I look up and see Saint marching across the barnyard, coming directly and intently toward me. He is alone. I look around inside the car, feel inside my pockets, find a few treats, and get out of the car. I close the door quietly because I don't want to alert Cherokee or Dahli Lama to my arrival. By now, Saint is already stationed at the fence, awaiting—demanding even—his customary treats. His herdmates are a good distance away, and I'm happy that once again, he has spotted and reached me first. No chance of his being pushed out of their way. It's just him and me and the cookies. He nibbles from one hand while I stroke him with the other.

Whether it was through Saint's in-person interactions with me, his messages after crossing over, or the images of him as they move across my memory's field of vision from time to time, ours was a joined journey with many powerful learnings. When we came into each other's lives, we were novices in regard to certain things. He had never had a special person to dote on him, and I was a demonstrative person who had never lived with a horse, let alone one who was challenged by showings of affection. But as his confidence and sense of security expanded, so too did my ability to sense what he needed in a given moment. And by the time our physical journey together had drawn to a close, we had spent several years enjoying an emotional, as well as a physical, closeness. I kissed and embraced him as I pleased, and he asked for cookies as *he* pleased. And now that he has crossed over, being able to connect with him telepathically has been an extraordinary experience.

In so many ways, our animal relatives are superb teachers, even from across the rainbow bridge. My telepathic connections with Saint have let me know that the arc of our relationship continues to shoot across time and space. And while it would be lovely to hug his orangey-brown furry neck once again, I gratefully embrace his presence in my life in whatever form it comes.

19

Circumambulations

After Hannah and Luis had finished their caretaking stints with me following the airborne riding misadventure with Cherokee, my recuperation and I were on our own. But from then on, Luis and I kept in touch. In fact, we kept in very close contact, talking on the phone on a near-daily basis. That was a new development in our relationship.

Over the next few months, things between us progressed, and by early July, we were dancing around the edges of an outright conversation about reuniting. Near the end of that month, we gingerly had "the talk." It was decided. We would come together again. As for the details of who, what, where, when, and how, only the *who* and *what* were clear. The last three remained moving targets for quite some time.

One day shortly after that conversation, I was talking to Luis on the telephone while standing in my front yard. A fully formed double rainbow suddenly appeared and majestically arched itself across the farmhouse property. When I described it to Luis, his immediate comment was, "That's you and me." I was deeply touched, not only by the sweetness of his sentiment, but also by the sound of happiness in his voice.

As the months passed, we spoke regularly by telephone. And while some of our chats were relatively lighthearted, on many occasions, my voice sounded heavy and morose, at least to my ears. As it turned out, it took two full years to get me back to the Empire State from the time we made the decision to reconcile. Especially in the final months of that period, I walked around with a heaviness of spirit, coupled with financial worry about finding an affordable property that the horses, dogs, and a reuniting human couple could call home. It was hard living physically in one place but emotionally in another. The sense of dissociation and disconnect was difficult to navigate, but Luis buoyed me as best he could.

Finally, we were able to purchase an eight-acre rural property that Luis and Elizabeth had checked out in Tivoli, a small village in Dutchess County, New York, roughly two and a half hours north of New York City. Since we were pinching every penny, nickel, and dime in the run-up to the move, I didn't fly east to check out the property firsthand. Still, the photographs posted on the real estate listing, as well as the videos shot by Luis and Elizabeth, all looked great. So it was two thumbs up from me all the way.

My two darling daughters had bookended me with their help in moving to and moving from Colorado. Elizabeth had accompanied me on my westward trek to Colorado and then stayed with me for five days before leaving me, like a babe in a basket, at the doorstep of the Rockies. Six years later, Hannah, who had moved to Colorado a couple of years after me, took over. She drove down from the mountains to help me pack and then load my menagerie and belongings into every square inch of a gooseneck trailer before sending me on my eastward trek back to New York.

Because finding the right horse transporter was an extremely sensitive issue for me, I had begun my research several months before Luis and I had even found a property to buy, let alone known where it would be or when we were likely to be in possession of it. I struck gold with Marlene Dodge, owner and founder of Valley View Ranch Equine Rescue, who happily agreed to be on standby and await my further timing updates. Even better, she offered to transport not only Cherokee and Dahli Lama but also Billy, Stitch, and me, plus all of my belongings. I didn't even know such an arrangement was possible, and I nearly cried with relief. I told her that she had lifted an immense weight off my heart because it had pained me to think of sending the horses off without me. All five of us were going to be able to stay together. Another joined journey.

Our spaces in the gooseneck trailer during the trip east were compact but comfortable. Marlene sat in the cab up front accompanied by Victoria, one of her interns. Stitch, Billy, and I traveled in the compartment behind them. And in another compartment behind us, Dahli Lama and Cherokee stood side by side, their heads facing in our direction of travel. All of my personal belongings were stashed high above us in an overhead cabin that was remarkably spacious.

I would be sleeping in my snug compartment, and my bed consisted of ten bales of hay stacked five atop five and covered by a sleeping bag. On the carpeted floor below me, there was just enough room to accommodate nearly two hundred pounds of pooch. It was endearing how willingly the two dogs accepted these limitations. It was also impressive that they still managed to do that classic spinning around thing that dogs so often do when readying themselves to plop down and relax.

Throughout the five-day, four-night journey, I kept my energy calm and my movements to a minimum to encourage the dogs to stay relaxed and still. They were true champions throughout, adapting beautifully to what must have been an odd and disorienting experience, even though their favorite human—me—was in close proximity.

Through the small slats in the door of our compartment, I took in as much as I could of the landscapes and terrains through which we were traveling. Much of it was highway travel—straight, flat, and uninspiring—though some parts of the journey did provide visual scenic relief, including the county fairgrounds we stayed at overnight. Each time we pulled into a fairground, I marveled at how skillfully Marlene maneuvered that huge trailer as she masterfully circled us around the narrow paths in the dark until we reached the areas where stables and outside corrals were located.

Forgoing the stalls, I let Cherokee and Dahli Lama spend their nights out in the corrals. Besides wanting to spare them the disconcerting experience of being confined in strange stalls, I also knew the crisp nighttime air of early October was heavenly for them. They enjoyed stretching, sniffing, standing around, and occasionally breaking into sprints, as well as catching their forty winks. During one especially memorable stopover at the Richmond County Fairgrounds in Mansfield, Ohio, the two of them romped and rolled through a couple of huge mud puddles, getting themselves nicely soil-encrusted from nose to tail. Meanwhile, tethered to a nearby tree with generously long ropes, Stitch and Billy breathed in the newness of their midwestern surroundings.

As for my *inner* topography, here too there were some extended patches of uninspired flatness. Perhaps it wasn't so much a lack of inspiration or contour as it was a matter of succumbing to a profound sense of relief that the move was finally underway. At the same time, a touch of bittersweetness also came into focus in my emotional landscape. For one thing, I was leaving behind a state and a town that had both been very good to me. I had ventured down spiritual, physical, and emotional pathways I felt certain I would not otherwise have discovered. And I was leaving behind a few wonderfully supportive friends. Neither Longmont nor Colorado had done me any wrongs. In returning to New York, my "spiritual directional" was a *getting back to* rather than a *getting away from*.

The trip was also tinged with bittersweetness because we were making it without Snuggle, Midnight, or Saint. Saint had crossed over a year earlier while the cats, then nearly nineteen years old, had been put down several months before that. It had been a year of three sad losses. Still, all three had been loved greatly and had lived long lives before being compassionately put down once their bodies were irrefutably failing them. For Billy and me, it was a return to the land of our respective births. For Stitch, Dahli Lama, and Cherokee, it represented a farewell to theirs and an embrace of a new one.

When Marlene pulled the trailer into the driveway in Tivoli

on October 4, it was late at night—too dark to see the property. As I climbed out of the compartment's side door and came
around the back of the trailer, I was a bit dazed and blinded by
the lights aimed at me from the headlamps Elizabeth, Hannah,
and Luis were wearing. Squinting, I walked into their lights
and hugged them, one at a time. After watching Marlene and
Victoria lead Dahli Lama and Cherokee into the enclosure Luis
had set up, I helped Luis and the girls lug bags, cases, and boxes
into the house. With every compartment of the trailer checked
by multiple sets of eyes, there was nothing left to do but pro-
fusely thank Marlene and Victoria and then watch them pull
back out into the darkness of unlit Lasher Road.

Much to my relief, Cherokee and Dahli Lama acclimated
quickly and well to their new digs. Although the property had
eight acres, only about half of them were fenced, and the barn
on site was in rather poor shape. After wavering between shell-
ing out big bucks for major repairs of that structure or making
alternate arrangements on the property, we opted for the latter.

We rented a shed row barn which, at the conclusion of the
four-year lease period, would have cost us roughly seventy percent over and above its actual price tag if bought outright. It
wasn't long before we discovered the distinct disadvantages of
setting a floorless structure directly down on a foundation-less
plot of wetland. Seeing the error of our ways, we relinquished
the barn after two months.

Over the course of the next several weeks, Luis and I con-
verted the ramshackle, unfinished chicken coop that had come
with the property into a two-stall barn with a decent-sized center aisle. While the finished product wouldn't have made the

cover of *Horse&Rider* magazine, it became a serviceable stable. True, we all—Cherokee, Dahli Lama, Luis, and I—had to make the best of certain less than ideal conditions, such as the leaking roof, the logistical difficulties of securing rails and gates to the available infrastructure, and the hodgepodge lighting setup that offended Luis, bless his craftsman's heart. He had fully intended to do a complete overhaul of the structure come spring.

For the first month or so in Tivoli, I thought things would work out beautifully for Cherokee and Dahli Lama on their new turf. The ground was still fairly dry when we arrived the first week of October. It hadn't yet revealed itself as the miserably soggy terrain it turned into for many months of the year when there was at least an inch of standing water on some parts of the property and even more in others. Some early winter rain and snowfall disclosed that reality all too clearly. I felt anxious and guilty. I wondered what we had gotten ourselves and the horses into.

In the end, the situation turned intolerably sour for the horses, or more accurately, intolerably wet, causing abscesses and lameness in the horses and guilt in me. My spirits sank. I had known beforehand that the property was designated a wetland property and that, as a prerequisite to securing a mortgage commitment, we would have to purchase pricey flood insurance. Those dual realities should have set off alarms and propelled me into making at least a cursory online search on the topic of how horses fare on wetland. At a minimum, it should have prompted me to broach the subject with Bill.

Normally, where my animal relatives were concerned, I was a diligent and thorough researcher. But in my desperation to get back East, I had somehow failed to educate myself properly about the potential pitfalls of bringing horses onto such terrain. By then, Luis and I had logged countless hours on the phone, trolling real estate websites together, and Luis had driven all over the Hudson Valley region checking out prospective properties.

Despite our best efforts, all of the arrangements we tried out proved unworkable. None of the options were likely to keep the horses sound and in good health. In fact, within a ten-month period, there were three abscess-lameness-poulticing episodes (two suffered by Dahli Lama and one by Cherokee). Fearing for the horses' well-being, the sinking feeling in the pit of my stomach became near-constant.

So almost five months after arriving, I made the unthinkable and heavyhearted decision to board the horses until we could situate ourselves on a new property. Not knowing how long it would take to achieve that only added to my distress. But since the immediate task was finding an acceptable barn for the horses, I concentrated all my energy on that. It didn't take me long to make my selection. It was located in Lagrangeville, about forty-five minutes south of Tivoli, straight down the Taconic Parkway.

A few weeks later, on one of the few days in March when there was no storm in progress, the trailer pulled out of our driveway and headed down Lasher Road with Dahli Lama and Cherokee aboard. As I watched, I was sick with dread, sorrow, and a searing sense of guilt. Then I turned around and keeled over, grabbing both knees to stay on my feet. I made my way over to the car while still hunched over, fell against the front passenger door, and held myself up by holding onto the sideview mirror. Elizabeth, who had taken the train up from Manhattan to lend emotional support, came over to me and tried to stand me upright. She probably wanted to embrace me, but I shrugged her away. I stayed like that for several minutes, listening to the awful keening sounds that were coming out of me.

As soon as I was able to get myself moving, we got in the car and headed over to the barn where the horses were to be boarded. Anxious to minimize the amount of time they might experience any sense of fear, abandonment, or betrayal, I wanted to get there before the trailer arrived. *I'm coming, Cherokee, I'm coming, Dahli Lama,* I sounded silently as we drove. When we got there, though, Cherokee and Dahli Lama were already out of the trailer and standing in a small corral by themselves.

The next chapter in our journey had begun. And for the first time since the three of us had come together, it was not a wholly joined one, at least not in the physical realm. I was crushed with guilt and fear, sadness and loss. Heartsick, I prayed for God to watch over us, help us, and keep us safe in body, mind, and spirit.

20

No Hay Mal
que por Bien no Venga

For over seven months, Dahli Lama and Cherokee boarded at the Lagrangeville barn. The first thing I shared with the barn owners as they showed me around their sixty-acre spread was that my sole reason for boarding my horses was the lack of any dry parcel of pasture where we lived. I told them how emotionally wrecked I was about Cherokee and Dahli Lama having suffered, between them, three separate abscess episodes accompanied by lameness within a ten-month period. The owners nodded sympathetically as I eyed a double paddock that sat up on an elevated part of the property and sloped slightly downward. It was perfect for rain drain. That field was the best and only choice to make. Fortunately, it was vacant and available.

Dahli Lama and Cherokee would be turned out for several hours during the day and then led back to their adjoining stalls which, sadly, were separated by thick wooden planks that afforded them little, if any, view of one another. I was told that for the first two or three days, the two of them would be turned out together in a small paddock that was attached to one side of the barn for ease of observation and haltering.

In the end, though, they were confined to that space for an entire week, eight to ten hours a day. That wouldn't have been a major concern in and of itself. But because of the copious amount of melting snow from a week's worth of nor'easter activity, that paddock, situated as it was at the receiving end of the property's sloping terrain, was an ankle-high muddy mess. All too soon, my choice of barn seemed anything but wise. Although both horses looked fine for the first six days, on the seventh one, Dahli Lama showed lame.

Angst and self-recrimination raged as I faced up to the truth, at least as I saw it, that I had betrayed the trust my horses had placed in me. The minute I saw Dahli Lama limping across the paddock to greet me, I called the owners and expressed my deep concern. Both of them were defensive and dismissive of my speculation that her condition was very likely a moisture-related abscess. Nevertheless, they agreed to poultice and wrap her foot for the next few days rather than leave the task for me to do during my nightly visits. They also started bringing both horses out to their double paddock for turnout the next day. Within days, my handsome girl was traveling much better.

Putting aside that inauspicious beginning, along with a few other issues that arose, Cherokee and Dahli Lama were adequately cared for during their stay. The hardest part of boarding them was knowing that they were confined to their box stalls for all but eight or nine hours out of every twenty-four-hour period and that they weren't even together the rest of the time. They could only see and smell each other through the few random slits and cracks in the horizontal wooden logs that made up the ceiling-high wall separating their stalls. I didn't know how Cherokee and Dahli Lama felt about that setup. I was never brave enough to ask either one of them, in part because I was afraid of what their respective responses might be. Ignorance wasn't necessarily bliss, but it *was* a compassionate form of self-care.

I visited them every day without fail, usually from around six to eight each evening. Especially at the beginning of the new arrangement, it was hard to walk away at the end of each visit. Oddly enough, it became even harder during the final weeks at the barn, perhaps because the end couldn't come soon enough for me by then.

The last thing I did at each visit was stand in the center aisle outside their stalls to engage in our nightly prayer ritual. But in the week or so prior to their departure, I changed things up slightly. Before prayers, I went into their stalls, first Cherokee's and then Dahli Lama's, to stand beside them and paint mental pictures of the moon passing across the sky several times, as well as images of the big fields they would soon be enjoying. Bill had suggested I do that whenever I needed to leave the horses for any extended period of time or when I wanted to convey any messages having to do with the passage of time.

While standing in front of Dahli Lama's stall one evening shortly before our stay at the barn was nearly at an end, I was reflecting on all the things I'd learned as a member of that barn community, and I was filled with gratitude. Then I heard in my mind one of my favorite Spanish-language expressions: *No hay mal que por bien no venga.* Loosely translated, it meant "There is

nothing bad from which good does not come." It was the equivalent of the English-language expression "Every cloud has a silver lining."

I grinned into space and thought that it was perfect that
the adage had come to me in that setting, gifting me with a
fresh perspective on the barn experience, one that was so much
healthier than the guilt-tainted one with which I'd been poison-
ing myself. I found myself reflecting upon some of those valuable takeaways which, in large part, consisted of improvements
to my somewhat irregular grooming habits.

I had developed and stuck to a routine that included numerous grooming tasks: picking their hooves; squirting diluted
bleach on their feet every few days to ward off thrush and other
hoof and foot maladies; currying from head to tail; removing
countless burdock burrs from forelocks, manes, and tails; checking them for cuts, scrapes, and bites; spraying them with bug
repellent when the torturous fly season descended; and spong-
ing them down when the day had been hot and sticky. I even
tried something new during the last month or so of their stay at
the barn: indoor showers. I had previously only taken a hose to
the horses while they were tied up outdoors, but the barn had
an enclosed washroom. Separately, I led them down the aisle
to that room, tethered them in a corner, and hosed them down
from nose to tail, withers to belly. They both handled it brilliant-
ly, and because it was an unseasonably hot October, they each
enjoyed three or four showers before their stay was over.

For the first month or so of their boarding, except for the
washroom showers, I did all the other grooming activities right
in their stalls. It was less than ideal working in such a confined

space, especially with Dahli Lama. Unlike her much calmer behavior when groomed in more commodious spaces, she was a bit jiggy when I picked her hooves in her stall. That made me nervous, so I decided to try cross-tying the horses in the center aisle, like most of the other boarders were doing with their horses. I had never tried that before, and I was both relieved and pleased at how well the three of us took to that practice.

Except for the one time when I tried to do things differently.

Up to that point, I had only let one horse at a time be cross-tied in the aisle. But one evening when I was the only human around and it was late enough that no one else was likely to show up, I got it into my head to take both horses out into the center aisle at the same time. I should have dismissed the idea as soon as it presented itself, but I had probably fallen prey to the sentimental notion that it would be sweet for the three of us to hang out together in the aisle. So I forged ahead.

I brought out Cherokee first and fastened his halter to the nearby set of crossties. Then I brought out Dahli Lama, whose halter I hitched to the crossties that were about twelve feet behind Cherokee. I had both horses facing in the same direction, so only Dahli Lama had a view of her herd mate, and then only his derriere.

I began grooming Cherokee while keeping a close watch on Dahli Lama and then switched to grooming Dahli Lama while keeping an eye on Cherokee. That I was a bit nervous about the setup should have made me reconsider what I was doing, but I continued to toggle between the two horses every minute or so.

Then, when I was working on Dahli Lama, I heard shuffling sounds from Cherokee and looked up in time to see him twisting and turning his head around just enough to free himself from his halter and the two chains attached to either side of it. Dahli Lama could see what was happening, and I was teetering somewhere between disbelief and panic as Cherokee was starting to turn around.

I left Dahli Lama and walked toward Cherokee, being careful to avoid approaching him with too much energy because it would risk increasing whatever adrenaline rush had already begun coursing through his veins. And for the few seconds during which I maintained that restrained gait, I actually felt a modicum of confidence that Cherokee might be willing to stay there while I made my approach. I just needed to get closer to him and position myself in a way that obstructed his view of the other end of the barn, because the barn doors were open.

Interestingly, right after I had the notion to bring both horses into the aisle for grooming, it had occurred to me that I should close the barn doors at the far end of the barn before bringing the horses out. But I dismissed the idea, thinking it was unnecessary—despite the fact that I had something of a healthy paranoia about horse gates or doors being left open or being improperly closed.

As I drew near his left side, my eyes darted around to see what, if anything, was within arm's reach to use as a lead to gingerly drape around his neck. But he turned fully around to his right, and without hesitation, he started walking toward those open barn doors. Still, by altering my course and walking to my right, I was at least positioned between him and the far end as he approached me. I tried to block his way—a little human trying to look huge enough to the big horse to maybe make him think he didn't have enough room to pass. It was an ineffectual, short-lived attempt. Without any fuss on his part, Cherokee simply sidestepped and walked past me, all the while maintaining his unhurried but intentional walking gait.

With my first two attempts at averting disaster a failure, I followed Cherokee without falling too far behind but also without gaining any ground. His lack of urgency, juxtaposed with my awareness of the potential for disaster and heartbreak, was disorienting and surreal. I scanned the wall to my left and grabbed the first halter and lead I saw hanging from a hook. Maybe, just maybe, I thought, I could step up my gait enough (without inspiring him to do the same) to come up alongside him and place the rope over his neck.

I picked up my pace a bit, but at that point, Cherokee was a mere ten or so feet from the opening—no more than a few easy equine strides. I watched as he walked through the open doorway and out into the unfenced world. There was nothing else I could do but follow in his hoofsteps. I stopped only long enough to close the sliding doors, knowing that I was leaving Dahli Lama alone in the barn, cross-tied and unable to follow us and also knowing that she wouldn't be able to see where either of us had gone. I was afraid she might hurt herself in a frenzied attempt to pull off her own Houdini escape. I wanted to put her back in her stall but knew there wasn't time for that.

Fortunately, it was springtime and therefore still light out. Cherokee started to head down the dirt path, and I followed several human paces behind him. I was helpless to do anything else. Clapp Hill Road was straight ahead of us about a hundred feet down the path. A massive wave of terror assaulted my

body, my mind—my entire being. I had the sickening realization that if Cherokee made it to the road, he could be struck by
a vehicle, and even if he wasn't killed, he could be maimed so
badly that I would have no choice but to put him down.

But lo and behold, Cherokee veered off to his left, went
down a small incline, and took himself into the small paddock
where he and Dahli Lama had spent their first week. Not only
was the paddock unoccupied at the time, but surprisingly, the
gate had been left wide open. With an expanse of limitless open
terrain available to him, that was the choice Cherokee made!

I followed him into the paddock, latched the gate behind
me, and stood there for half a minute or so, breathing in the
miracle of the moment. It was over! He and I were both okay!

Meanwhile, Cherokee had moseyed over to the other side
of the paddock. Watching him nibble away at a patch of grass,
I felt a surge of gratitude that at least *one* of us had not been
gripped by fear and dread for the last several minutes. Clearly,
it hadn't been a big deal for him, let alone an ordeal.

But then I became aware of Dahli Lama's cries, and they
told me it *was* an ordeal for her. She was alarmed. I draped
the halter and lead over the top rail of the paddock fence and
headed back to the barn at a trot, praying that my girl hadn't
been straining at the chains on either side of her face vigorously
enough to have injured herself.

Once I got to her and gave her a quick once-over, I saw that
there were no signs of physical injury. But her eyes told a different story about her emotional state. They were on high alert,
pupils laser-like with apprehension. I stroked the left side of her
neck and murmured my apologies. Then I fastened a rope to

her halter, released the crossties, and walked her into her stall. I left her with a bowl of grain pellets, filled my jacket pockets with more, and headed back out to Cherokee. I felt bad that Dahli Lama would have to make do with this half-measure of relief, but I had no choice.

Once I was back inside the small paddock with Cherokee, I held out my hand in a gesture conveying that I had treats. He came right over and was easily haltered. Walking back to the precious mare, I made a silent promise to myself, to the universe, and to Spirit: *After this, I will never complain about anything, ever again. Anything!* I'd made that vow many times before and, of course, had failed to keep it. But feeling such immense relief and gratitude that this terrifying episode hadn't ended in disaster, there it was being offered up again, that same promise. And just like every other time, I *meant* it.

The next several months included selling the Tivoli property, starting a new high-pressure job, putting in twelve-to-fourteen-hour days involving home-to-work-to-barn-to-home commutes, finding a new place for all of us, and securing a mortgage. I was disappointed that my equine coaching work would have to stay on hold for a while longer but relieved that Luis and I were prioritizing the welfare of the horses. Finally, the day arrived when we were all reunited. With Luis, me, and the dogs sharing our new home, and Cherokee and Dahli Lama sharing their new barn, we were blessed to be living together on a wonderful eleven-acre rural spread in Pine Bush, New York, an hour due west of the Hudson River. A sweet paradise.

Grace, luck, know-how, and karma all seem to play their roles in life's happenings and unfoldings, but in what measures?

Can such elements even *be* measured? Need they be? In the end, life is a bit of a mystery dance. We curtsy, we bow, we sway, we dip. Sometimes we move with grace and flow, and sometimes we lose our balance and stumble or maybe even fall down on the dance floor. But we get back up, shake off the dust and embarrassment, tune back into the rhythm of the music, and start dancing again. Along the way, we gain a few inklings of insight. Cha-cha-cha.

No hay mal que por bien no venga. Amén.

21

Serendipitous Journey

What unseen forces had conspired, what invisible threads had been woven to transport me from the Empire State (New York) to the Centennial State (Colorado) and back again?

Taking a look back at the long arc of one's life is like looking at the surface of a mountain. Standing on the ground some distance away from a mountain, the perspective is that of "the big picture." The sides slope upward and meet at the peak. The peak might be pointy or blunt, but the slopes meet there. If it's a range of mountains, then there may be overlapping slopes. Still, the view is that of slopes and peaks, slopes and peaks.

But if we endeavor to take stock of a time in our life while actually living *through* it, the perspective is so different. We're *on* the mountain, climbing it rather than viewing it from the ground. We're keenly aware of the multitudinous contours, textures, and ridges, and we're aware of the many times we've had to change direction to avoid this or that risky footing or to gain a more efficient way to ascend or descend. Sometimes we halt the climb to just pause and take in the view or to reassess our intended goal.

A year or so after moving to Pine Bush, I was heading home from a day of writing at a café in the neighboring town of Gardiner. I took a new route, and as I rounded a curve, the vista opened to a view of the Wallkill River. In fact, the car was heading straight for it. The road was practically level with the riverbank, so the glistening sight was close up and personal. Beckoning too. I parked the car and sat myself down a few feet away from and above the water.

The practice of allowing the listening to extend to the farthest sound came to mind, so as I watched the flow of the river, I let the thoughts that arose fall away, returning my attention to the sounds of nature, again and again. Observing the sunlight play upon the countless surfaces of the river, I was grateful for the fleeting moments that I was free of thought and one with the listening.

It was a late January afternoon and quite breezy. The water was running swiftly. The phrase, "watch the shape of things" once again came to mind. As the fast-moving water flowed swiftly by me, from left to right, I experienced the tension and the dance being created by the river, adamant and insistent that its current be allowed to move in one direction while being resisted and opposed by the wind blowing fiercely back against the water. I could see the results of that tension between two mighty forces in the form of marvelous patterns of rippling mini waves repeatedly surging up and crashing down. The sound was equally enthralling, and during the occasional lulls in the wind, I was treated to the sweet sounds of gurgling river babble.

As much as I appreciated the quietening of the usual mental chatter, I did allow some insights to have their say. It occurred to me that the daily near-constant agitations of one's mind were being perfectly reenacted by the scene unfolding before me. Any day's events could be represented by the river, which was simply flowing along in its natural direction when left unimpeded. But the mind, full of hot air, blows onto the scene with its habitual impeding forces: *Well, okay, this is happening. It's fine, I guess. But wouldn't it be even better if this or that* (whatever preferable scenario the mind conjured) *happened?* Or *Why is this happening? Everything was just fine a minute ago, now this.*

After a while, those contemplations shifted and I was presented with a different takeaway to glean from the wind-and-river show I was watching. Perhaps the water flowing in one direction represented our habitual desire to keep things as they are, to hold at bay any change to the status quo. The gusting winds might be all the life circumstances that invariably come our way to threaten that status quo, nudging—sometimes hurling—us out of our comfort zones. *What a marvelous teacher Nature is!* I thought.

Our inner nature is equally marvelous. Some years ago, during my training in the TBAH coaching program, I spontaneously proclaimed my mission statement to a fellow student: I live to light the spark of awareness in others of the light within them. That statement represents my inner nature, my soul's life purpose, and there are many ways that mission expresses itself in my life. Sometimes the opportunity arises during a simple quotidian activity such as a conversation with an acquaintance, new or old. I see something to praise about that person and take a moment to share my awareness. Other ways require a bit more orchestration, such as planning and facilitating a therapeutic coaching session.

Every day, we're presented with opportunities to remind one another of the divine spark that glows within each of us. And in reminding others, we remind ourselves as well. It happens every time we make a heart-to-heart connection through words, actions, telepathy, or other channels.

One of the most natural ways we remind one another is through storytelling. I believe we all instinctively recognize our deep need to listen to stories and to tell them. I think of storytelling as a spiritual imperative, an integral part of how we help ourselves and others get a handle on this full catastrophe (as Nico Kazantzakis' Zorba the Greek put it) that is life.

Which of the stories we tell and which of the stories we listen to will result in altering the trajectory of someone else's life or our own. In archery, we nock our arrow, extend with one arm and pull back with the other, inhale, drop our shoulders, exhale, and release. Where the arrow lands is literally out of our hands. And for a few precious moments, we have an utter lack of control as to the outcome. It is left to us to stand and bear witness, to watch and wait. *To watch the shape of things.*

Mine is the story of a serendipitous journey that began taking shape with one enchanting creature, the horse. But of course, there's no limit to what might inspire the journeys we take or the stories we share. We all have synchronicities, serendipities, and magical connections being woven into our lives. Acknowledging and honoring those that come into our awareness creates space for new possibilities, pathways, and portals to reveal themselves. And isn't that what life is—a journey that we are in a constant state of joining?

As we sit at the feet of our teachers, gurus, and spiritual leaders, gratefully receiving their guidance, let us remember, too, that the capacity to seek out and discover those pathways and portals lies within each of us.

May we all embark on the spirit rides that beckon.
May we all gain a deep and abiding trust
In what those inward and outward travels reveal and teach.
May we all return home to ourselves and others
with myriad tales to be told.
Aho! So mote it be! Amen!

Afterword

It's just a walk into another pasture.

On a brisk and sunny October afternoon in Pine Bush, I decided to see if Dahli Lama wanted to engage with me telepathically. The day before, I had been one of six women in an online sacred circle, engaging in rich discussions about the interplay of logic, emotion, and intuition and sharing stories of communication with animals and other sentient beings. That two-hour event had inspired me to check in with my lovely mare the next day.

I bundled up and took some carrots and apple chunks out to the barn and fed them to Dahli Lama and Cherokee. Then I walked a short distance away so they would know that no more treats were forthcoming. I pulled up a chair and sat down outside the rails, noticing that both horses had decided to hang out in the corral area rather than go out to one of the fields or back into the barn.

Closing my eyes, I connected to my body in the chair, my feet on the ground, the play of air on my face, and the sounds all around me (and within me, thanks to the continuous tinnitus hum I've been living with these past several years). I brought an image of Dahli Lama to mind and started up the conversation. For some reason, what I chose to share with her was my desire for us to stay connected, not just soul to soul but also physically, as we were now. Tears had formed behind my closed eyes.

I thought I heard her tell me then that this (death) was a topic for another time. But that must not have been accurate on my part because what appeared in my mind's eye moments later was a series of images that conveyed valuable lessons to me about that very topic. It was a repeating moving image of a dark grey horse's rear end and hind legs. Each repetition showed the horse walking away from me. The imagery was on a loop, with each walk away lasting only two or three seconds.

I was aware that it was Dahli Lama and also that she was walking from one pasture into another. Intuitively, I knew that she was showing me how to view death, how to both understand and be at peace with it. Then I heard *It's just a walk into another pasture*, and I was certain that this was her message to me about death.

After numerous repetitions, the moving images stopped, and the final "walk away" dissolved into a still image of that same dark grey rear end. But this time, it had a heart shape right in the center of it. Three words formed in my mind: Heart. Root. Repeat. And I flashed back to the chakra alignments Dahli Lama had performed on me up at Kesa Ranch when she was still a yearling. With those words came the insight that she was showing me another way to embrace the life-death-life cycle. I could see life as heart and root, over and over again. All that was needed was for me to ground myself in the knowledge that love was the source of all, the one true energetic force that connected us all, across time, space, place, dimensions, and multiverses. Love was the portal.

After this, I became aware that Dahli Lama wanted me to sit quietly while she checked in with my chakras. So I sat there and let her guide me to relax this and that body part as I wept a bit. I noticed a tightness in my jaw area, so I opened my mouth and began moving it and my tongue around in a leaching sort of way. It felt instinctive and releasing.

Soon after this, I offered up thanks to Dahli Lama and to Spirit for all that had just taken place. The session had organically brought itself to a close.

The words and images that Dahli Lama presented to me about physical death have influenced my perspective on a reality I've striven for decades to embrace with greater understanding and grace. My willingness to reflect on and begin integrating this huge lesson didn't surprise me because I have learned to trust what I see, hear, feel, and know during heart-to-heart connections with animals, trees, and other creatures.

All sentient beings have stories to share, lessons to teach, and support to offer. We have only to open our hearts and say, *Ahh.*